No. 2
Brief Lives
QUEEN VICTORIA

Brief Lives

QUEEN VICTORIA IN 1897
THE YEAR OF HER DIAMOND JUBILEE

QUEEN VICTORIA

By
ROGER FULFORD

BRIEF LIVES
COLLINS, ST JAMES'S PLACE
LONDON

FIRST PUBLISHED 1951
THIS EDITION 1955

*The extracts from Queen Victoria's diary
and letters are made by permission from
"The Letters of Queen Victoria"
published by John Murray*

PRINTED IN GREAT BRITAIN
COLLINS CLEAR-TYPE PRESS: LONDON AND GLASGOW

CONTENTS

ILLUSTRATIONS

* 1 *

Princess Victoria

THE LOT of children in Nineteenth Century England was neither happy nor enviable, for they were brought up with a bleak severity which can be quickly appreciated by reading the novels of the time. The old saying (which was very popular in Victorian households) that children should be seen and not heard expresses only a partial truth. For it was more than just being seen. In those days children were observed, discussed, criticised or approved by the grown-ups, while they were expected to sit or stand before these voluble elders in mute deference, like a blushing waxwork at Madame Tussaud's. Their food was ample but rough, they were given the smallest, most inaccessible and chilliest rooms in the house, their medicines were horrible but regularly administered. Relations between them and their parents were stiffly affectionate and were marked by advice, reprimand and slap in confusing and rapid succession. Their chief protection lay in their numbers; like nestlings they kept each other secure, and minimised the severities of their surroundings by sharing them. Harsh indeed was the lot of an only child at this time! Although Queen Victoria had a stepbrother and stepsister, they were many years older than she so that the Queen virtually belonged to that sad and solitary class of only children. From the austerities which were characteristic of her age and generation royal rank did little to protect her.

She was born in 1819, on May 24th, and was christened, in the following June, Alexandrina Victoria. Her father, the Duke of Kent, one of those noisy and remarkable but gifted sons of King George III, was an advanced Liberal and he chose the first name out of compliment to Czar Alexander of Russia who, in those days, was the rather unexpected hero of English Liberals and Radicals. At first some efforts were made to call her by this name and she was known in the family circle as Drina, but when she passed from infancy to childhood she was called by her second name— though occasionally in the Gallic form of Victoire. This name was given her after her mother—a princess of the royal house of Saxe-Coburg and a sister of King Leopold of the Belgians—that sagacious and devoted uncle whom the Queen adored.

The first winter of the Queen's life was exceptionally cold, and during it the thermometer recorded as much as 16 degrees of frost. The infant Vic-

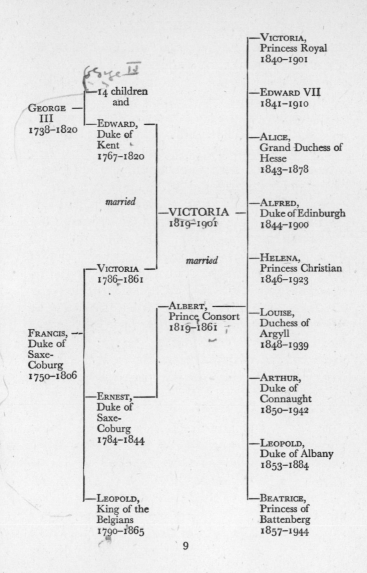

George IV

GEORGE III
1738–1820
— 14 children
and
— EDWARD,
Duke of
Kent
1767–1820

married

FRANCIS,
Duke of
Saxe-
Coburg
1750–1806
— VICTORIA
1786–1861

— ERNEST,
Duke of
Saxe-
Coburg
1784–1844

— LEOPOLD,
King of the
Belgians
1790–1865

— VICTORIA
1819–1901

married

— ALBERT,
Prince Consort
1819–1861

— VICTORIA,
Princess Royal
1840–1901

— EDWARD VII
1841–1910

— ALICE,
Grand Duchess of
Hesse
1843–1878

— ALFRED,
Duke of Edinburgh
1844–1900

— HELENA,
Princess Christian
1846–1923

— LOUISE,
Duchess of
Argyll
1848–1939

— ARTHUR,
Duke of
Connaught
1850–1942

— LEOPOLD,
Duke of Albany
1853–1884

— BEATRICE,
Princess of
Battenberg
1857–1944

9

toria's grandfather, King George III, who had for nine years been insane and was over eighty, died as a result of the weather after calling out, in his incoherent way, " Tom's a cold." Unhappily the Duke of Kent, in spite of spending the winter under the benign skies of Devonshire, likewise caught cold and died as a result of inflammation of the lungs a few days before his father.

Queen Victoria had a highly developed sense of what was spectacular and dramatic, referring to herself as " the poor fatherless baby of eight months." Though poignant, this description was not, of course, inaccurate: and the death of her father was a particular calamity for her since, deprived of him, she had to endure an excess of petticoat government. Until she was eighteen, when she became Queen, she always slept in the same bedroom with her mother, and as a child her companions were chiefly the elderly ladies who formed her mother's diminutive court. Royal persons, whose opportunities for making friends and enjoying society are often more severely limited than the public imagines, not infrequently lead lives of surprising dullness and seclusion. The widowed Duchess showed that this was so in her case when, in a speech in the City of London referring to the days of Queen Victoria's infancy, she said, " We stood alone, almost friendless and unknown in this country. I could not even speak the language of it." In addition, the Duchess, who was agreeable though not always wise, believed that children should be brought up with Spartan severity. Queen Victoria's half-sister—and she was certainly not exaggerating—described the Queen's early life as " that dismal existence " and " those years of imprisonment." When she came to the throne, Queen Victoria said she never wanted to eat mutton again, as she had had a surfeit of this food as a girl.

The Queen was brought up in Kensington Palace —the large and splendid Wren building at the western end of Hyde Park. King George II was the last sovereign to live here and at the beginning of the nineteenth century it had been divided into several suites of apartments, in one of which Queen Victoria was born; the others were occupied by her uncles and aunts—the younger children of King George III. These fast-fading, elderly persons loved their gay little niece, and a visit to them was one of her principal relaxations. Her other great consolation was the delightful grounds by which the Palace was surrounded. They merged into what is now Kensington Gardens. The future Queen loved the freedom of these walks and lawns and was often seen there, riding on a donkey followed, at a respectful distance, by a footman in crimson livery. (In those days the servants of the sovereign alone were entitled to wear scarlet.)

When she was only five the Princess was handed

over to the care of a governess—that devoted, most formidable and industrious German lady—the Baroness Lehzen. With an ugly voice, a yellow skin and a habit of perpetually sucking caraway seeds, she was not precisely attractive but she made up for her lack of charm by an affection for her pupil which was both touching and profound. When she was a middle-aged woman, the Queen looking back to the days of her childhood, wrote of Lehzen, " She was an admirable governess, and I adored her, though I also feared her." In addition to the Baroness, the Princess had a tutor, whom she made a bishop when she came to the throne, and a number of visiting masters. Her education, at any rate in its early stages, was largely based on the books of a worthy lady called Mrs. Trimmer— an eighteenth-century matron who had once been favourably noticed by Dr. Johnson. She was really the pioneer of teaching children by picture books, and almost all her publications were carefully studied by the Princess. Mrs. Trimmer's books were richly sprinkled with good advice and moral precepts. For example, in her *Introduction to the Knowledge of Nature*, she warns her readers against eating green gooseberries, illustrating this warning by the story of a little boy who ate some and then " he entirely lost his appetite, and his rosy cheeks became as pale as death; at last worms, live worms, came into his bowels." Mrs. Trimmer also wrote story books, and the Queen was said to have been very fond of *The Story of the Robins*, with its four characters who were given the somewhat unoriginal names of Robin, Dicky, Flapsy and Pecksy. Although it is easy enough to laugh at the innocent moralisings of Mrs. Trimmer they have their place in any understanding of the Queen's character. Certainly the Queen was no scholar and, in childhood, she was naughty, reluctant to learn and too often bored by her lessons.

By nature the Queen was extraordinarily straightforward, truthful and direct; she was not subtle for she always wrote and said exactly what was in her mind. That makes her, in many ways, a surprisingly easy character to understand. But this particular trait of straightforwardness in her character was strengthened by her upbringing and by her grounding in the works of Mrs. Trimmer. Her family obviously set great store by strength of character as can be seen from this sentence in a letter which her uncle, King Leopold, wrote to her :

" Nothing in persons gives greater reliance," he wrote, " greater weight than when they are known to be true." But anyone who supposes that Queen Victoria was a sort of George Washington in petticoats will be grievously wide of the mark. Although she was always obstinately accurate and truthful, her character was softened by her gaiety and high spirits. Moreover she had a great variety of accomplishments. Her natural powers of description were carefully developed by her instructors and she was able to express herself with the pen gracefully and quickly. She was musical, and she could draw with a skill which was far above the average. Although she was small, about five feet, two inches high (she said once " I am rather short for a Queen "), she walked with a dignity which compelled attention. She always danced beautifully and her grace of movement came from her tuition in the arts of the ballroom, thereby recalling the truth of Pope's familiar line:

"As those move easiest who have learned to dance."

Her education, while strengthening her character, had perhaps developed her accomplishments without stretching her intellect. She was acutely conscious of the gaps in her knowledge and she once told her husband that she did not like to be left too long in conversation with a single individual in case the gaps in what she knew became obvious. When she came to the throne she said rather pathetically to her Prime Minister:

" I often feel so conscious of saying stupid things in conversation, and I often think I am very childish."

The prospect of ascending the throne, which became a certainty when King William IV's infant children died, would not seem to have unduly disturbed the Princess's childhood or to have unduly oppressed her. When she was nine years old, Sir Walter Scott saw her at Kensington. The great romantic novelist was a firm Tory and he disapproved of her Christian name—expressing the hope that it might be changed, because it had not previously been the name of a member of the English Royal Family. So prevalent was this feeling that a few years afterwards the House of Commons solemnly debated whether her Christian name should not be changed to Charlotte. Sir Walter added that if the fair little head of the Princess could have been dissected, the brain would show that someone had already whispered to her that she would one day be Queen. Reading this passage in later life, the Queen commented that Sir Walter was quite wrong and that at that time she had no idea of what was in store for her. The matter was finally explained to her, when she was thirteen, by Baroness Lehzen who slipped a family tree into the Princess's history book. The familiar story that she commented " I will be good " (though not inaccurate) makes her out slightly pompous and priggish which was never in keeping with her character. Nor indeed would such words come naturally to a girl in her early teens. What she in fact said was this:

" I am nearer than I thought. I see now why you always wanted me to work well at my lessons. I will be good."

She meant of course that she would try to be good at her lessons—but she was not referring, as is often implied, to the vast field of responsibility which was opening before her. On that prospect she always looked calmly—and even with a certain detached good humour. When she was fifteen her uncle sent her an extract from a French book which contained a severe attack on Queen Anne. The Princess immediately wrote back thanking him for telling her what a Queen ought not to be and asking that he would now quickly let her know what a Queen ought to be. And a few years later, when it was obvious that King William IV was dying and that the Princess would imminently become Queen, she wrote to her uncle:

"I look forward to the event, which it seems is likely to occur soon, with calmness and quietness: I am not alarmed at it, and yet I do not suppose myself quite equal to it."

* 2 *

The Young Queen

King William IV expired at Windsor Castle at two o'clock in the morning on June 20th. He loathed the Duchess of Kent and once publicly expressed the hope that he might live till his niece was eighteen, when she would be of age and capable of reigning without the necessity for a Regent, who would have been her mother. This wish was gratified and the Princess was eighteen and one month when she came to the throne. As soon as the King was dead, the Lord Chamberlain, who is the head of the Royal Household, and the Archbishop of Canterbury mounted their horses and set out from Windsor, through the summer night, for Kensington Palace. They arrived at six in the morning and after knocking up sleepy servants they were received by the Princess, alone in her sitting-room, wearing her dressing-gown. The Lord Chamberlain explained that the King had died, and he then dropped on his knees and kissed the hand of the young Queen. With characteristic presence of mind she told him to tell the King's widow, as soon as he got back to Windsor, how deeply she felt for her.

For the Queen her accession to the throne was more than a change—it was a break, complete and decisive, with her old life. The bluff, outspoken uncle, lying white and still on his death-bed in the Blue Room at Windsor Castle, had lived just sufficiently long to enable her not only to be Queen but to be mistress of her own life. The thralldom of the mother was broken. No more was that devoted but foolish lady to occupy the Queen's bedroom: no more was she to guide her daughter's every action and to restrain her every impulse: no more was she to hem her in with stuffy companions of her own choosing. The Queen was free. In her journal describing the events of that historic morning, the Queen explains that she saw the Lord Chamberlain and the Archbishop *alone.* The reader can almost sense the emphasis and relief with which the Queen underlined that word. Three hours later she saw her Prime Minister, Lord Melbourne, and again in her journal she underlines the words " *of course quite alone.*" Yet if she was plainly elated and jubilant, the ordeal of that day was formidable in the extreme—especially for one who had seen little of affairs and next to nothing of men. At half-past eleven she had to meet the Privy Council—a gathering of some fifty or sixty peers and leading politicians—in the Red Saloon at Kensington Palace. There was a large attendance because of people's curiosity to know what she was like. She came in alone, a diminutive but graceful figure in black, and her two uncles—the Dukes of Cumberland and Sussex—rose to greet her and lead her to her place. She read a short speech in that beautiful, bell-like voice which was to charm generations of English politicians, and then the men filed up one by one to kiss her hand. The chorus of praise was immediate. " She was perfection," wrote one diarist. A former Lord Chancellor grumbled at her because in her speech she used the word " amelioration ": he said, " I object to her grammar: she ought to have said ' improvement.' " But she won the hearts of her distinguished audience — Whigs and Tories alike — by her remarkable combination of modesty and self-possession. Her manner throughout was perfectly natural and easy. As soon as the Council was over, the Master of the Horse, who was responsible for all the royal coaches and carriages, came to see her. He kissed her hand and asked what orders she had to give him. She laughed and said that he knew so much more about it than she did that she would leave it to him, but that she must have a proper conveyance to take her to St. James's Palace the following day.

Throughout that day she constantly saw her Prime Minister Lord Melbourne, and after their last conference in the evening she referred to her confidence in him and to his kindness. Though Lord Melbourne was certainly not the greatest of Queen Victoria's Prime Ministers, he was indubitably the most human, and of them all the one by whom a young girl would have asked to be tutored. He was a Whig though not a rabid party man, and his reaction to most reforms is characterised by his familiar question " Why can't you leave it alone? " He was not over-industrious but extremely astute. He was very widely read and in conversation full of witticisms and dry humour. He had been a member of the brilliant circle of the Prince Regent, and married to the dazzling but erratic Lady Caroline Lamb (the lover of Lord Byron); he was familiar with the world—a fact of which he constantly reminded the Queen. For her part she delighted in the gaiety and humour with which he tackled even the weightiest of official business. For example, in an official letter to the Queen, writing of the squabbles of servants, he said, " neither the Deity nor the Devil, nor both together, can make them agree." On another occasion, at a public function, it was necessary to make some slight change in the Queen's clothes. Afterwards she asked Lord Melbourne if he did not think it very embarrassing for her. He said at once:

" You might have said, ma'am, as Mary, Queen of Scots said before the scaffold ' I am not accustomed to be undressed before so many people, by such attendants.' " As the months passed, the Queen relied increasingly on Melbourne: her affection for him was deep and her confidence in him unbounded. For his part he gave an increasing amount of his time to the Queen and less to the routine engagements and discussions which are inseparable from the life of an active politician. To some it seemed that he gave more time to helping the Queen than to his duties as Prime Minister. In the House of Lords, Lord Brougham—a man of most varied gifts, fearless and eccentric—did not hesitate to give expression in public to what he regarded as Melbourne's debasement through preoccupation with Court affairs. In the course of a debate on a royal topic Brougham, referring to Melbourne, said:

" On a point of this sort I humble myself before my noble friend. I have no courtier-like cultivation. I am rude of speech. The tongue of my noble friend is so well hung, and so well attuned to courtly airs that I can not compete with him. I am not given to glozing and flattery." " Glozing " was a curious but expressive word, which was popular with the early Victorians for describing a flatterer. Melbourne made an effective and amusing reply, but the debate illustrated how even the House of Lords did not hesitate to criticise the Court and how jealousy of the royal house was still openly, and freely, expressed. Only seven years earlier, when Queen Victoria's uncle King George IV had died, *The Times* (though it was published with the deepest of black edges) wrote:

" The truth is, however—and it speaks volumes about the man,—that there never was an individual less regretted than this deceased King. What eye has wept for him? " The risks of attacks and lampoons on the Queen, possibly whipping up public opinion to make her really unpopular, was a very real danger in these early days of her reign. For that reason the shrewd and genial direction of her life by Melbourne was an inestimable advantage.

She was also greatly helped in the opening months of her reign by the Baron Stockmar—a German who was the confidential friend and adviser of her uncle, King Leopold. As soon as the Queen's accession became clearly imminent, King Leopold sent Stockmar across the channel to England. The real problem to settle was about the Queen's private secretary. The Queen offered the position to Stockmar but he wisely declined it because of being a foreigner. The Cabinet was nervous that a private secretary, with knowledge and experience of affairs, would gain complete control of the young Queen and might create difficulties between her and her Ministers. This had in fact happened in the reign of George IV. The problem was solved in characteristically English fashion by the device of appointing nobody. Melbourne became her adviser and secretary on all public matters, while Lehzen took over matters connected with the Court. Stockmar remained in the background—rather German and ponderous, but faithful, sensible and cautious. It will not be unnoticed that in all these arrangements the Duchess of Kent had no place. She lived, of course, with the Queen, taking her natural place on all social occasions; and those who came to dine at Buckingham Palace or Windsor Castle used to find her very agreeable if a trifle drowsy as night drew on, but from the working side of the Queen's life she was strictly excluded.

The work of an English sovereign at this time was heavy: much of it was responsible and some of it was delicate. There was to begin with a great deal of signing—routine measures of the Government were signed by the Queen—likewise all commissions for officers in the Armed Forces and a great variety of appointments—official, legal and ecclesiastical. Important despatches to foreign countries were approved by the Queen and all important issues of policy—both home and foreign—had to have the sanction of the Queen. Naturally enough a girl of eighteen could hardly be expected to have any valuable contribution to make on issues of high policy, and it was here that the Queen entirely followed the advice and guidance of Melbourne. But there were of course some matters—often rather delicate—in which the Queen—though advised—had to play her own part. For example, she had only been on the throne for a very few months when the Russian Ambassador resigned and asked for the customary audience of the sovereign on leaving England. The Foreign Secretary advised the Queen to be very careful what she said—especially about the Emperor of Russia, who was known to be very anxious for any excuse to visit the Queen—a compliment which the British Government particularly wanted to avoid. In all matters of this kind—where tact and discretion were needed—the Queen, though so young, showed to very great advantage and won the unstinted admiration of her ministers and advisers.

But although the Queen worked steadily, she had plenty of time for recreation. In fact the English Court, which under the Georges had always been rather dull and stuffy, suddenly became very gay. Nor would it be altogether an exaggeration to say that not since the days of Charles II had such high spirits reigned in an English palace. Some of the Queen's ladies-in-waiting were little older than herself and, in addition to formal Court balls which were frequently held, the Queen enjoyed small private dances with her friends when she whirled and waltzed with the greatest zest and energy until three o'clock in the morning or later. Lord Melbourne was frequently an amused spectator of these festivities as is shown by the following letter to him from the Queen:

" The Queen anxiously hopes Lord Melbourne has slept well, and has not suffered from last night. It was very wrong of him not to wish the Queen good-night, as she expected he would in so small a party. . . . When did he get home? It was great pleasure to the Queen that he came last night. We kept up the dancing till past three, and the Queen was much amused, and slept soundly from four till half past ten, which she is ashamed of. . . ."

For exercise she rode on horseback either in the Park when the Court was at Buckingham Palace or in Windsor Great Park when she was at the Castle. She had two favourite horses " my darlings " she called them. One was an Irish horse called Tartar, and the other—a chestnut " with a beautiful little Arabian head "—was called Uxbridge.

But neither the exacting nature of the work which the Queen had to do nor the gaiety of her hours of relaxation should be allowed to hide one other aspect of the sovereign's duties which she performed with great taste and brilliance. Those were her public and ceremonial appearances in London. A King or Queen of England, however hard he or she might work in the seclusion of Buckingham Palace, would rapidly become unpopular unless the work was accompanied by frequent appearances in public. One of the reasons why King George IV had been disliked was because the public never saw him. He lived in seclusion at Windsor. Naturally enough the public curiosity to see Queen Victoria—so youthful and yet bearing such a weight of responsibility—was enormous. Her first important ceremony was on November 9th—Lord Mayor's Day, when she drove in state to the City. The procession was huge and brilliant; it began with her mother and her uncles and aunts who each set out in one of those beautifully painted and brightly varnished nineteenth-century carriages with an escort of cavalry. The Queen sat on the back seat of the State Coach alone: the Master of the Horse and her closest personal friend the Duchess of Sutherland, who was Mistress of the Robes, sat facing her. As the procession turned out of Buckingham Palace, the private carriages of the Foreign Ambassadors and of members of the Government joined in behind the Queen's coach. Though the weather behaved with characteristic November dreariness, the people of London received the Queen with enthusiastic acclamation. At Temple Bar she was met by the Lord Mayor and the Aldermen of the City. These gentlemen—perhaps better at eating and drinking than at anything else in life—then clambered on to horses and rode with the Queen into the heart of the City. They were wearing their scarlet gowns, and their chains of office swung round their necks. Their horses had been well exercised and the

Aldermen contrived to cling on to their steeds with safety and without complete loss of dignity. Save for one. He attempted to bow to a lady who was watching from a window, fell heavily on to the gravel with which the street had been sprinkled, and his horse walked over him. The banquet with which the Queen was entertained at Guildhall was lavish and an enormous crowd of people sat down with her. When the Queen entered, the band struck up "O the Roast Beef of Old England." She sat at a special table between two of her uncles, who no doubt explained the various customs and described the guests to her. She made no speech but when her health was drunk she rose and bowed several times with the greatest grace and dignity. She took a fan with her, which at that time was as essential for a lady as a handbag is to-day; and unfortunately this fan caught the wine glass, in which she was about to drink the Lord Mayor's health, and broke it. She was greatly distressed by what she had done.

In the following June, when she was just nineteen, Queen Victoria was crowned. On the morning, with some lack of consideration, the Artillery began firing their guns in the Park at four o'clock. This woke the Queen and she had little sleep, thereafter, but she got up at seven feeling, as she said "strong and well." She had a little breakfast, dressed in her robes, and then a little breakfast again. When she set out for Westminster Abbey she noticed that great as had been the crowd when she drove to the City in the previous November, there were thousands more people on the route on this occasion. She did not apparently feel nervous—only, as she wrote, " proud to be the Queen of *such* a nation." When she was about half-way to the Abbey one of the traces of the State Coach broke and the Queen was delayed for five minutes. Her mother, when she was in the procession in the Abbey, realised that something must have gone wrong and left her place to wait for the Queen in the porch. The Duchess was overcome with relief when she saw her daughter and burst into floods of tears. Unperturbed by this rather distressing welcome to the Abbey, the Queen played her part with her customary quiet dignity.

The ceremony itself was of almost infinite duration as the Queen left Buckingham Palace at eleven and did not get back till six. The proceedings were ill-rehearsed and the Queen once or twice asked what she was to do next, but the Bishop, who was standing next to her, had to say that he did not know. But as always with Queen Victoria, it was the perfectly natural things she did which won the hearts of those watching. When her uncle, the Duke of Sussex, came to do his homage she got up, flung her arms round his neck and gave him a warm kiss. When an octogenarian peer, staggering under the weight of his robes, fell, she immediately left the throne to help him up. The Archbishop, with the clumsiness characteristic of one who has been an Oxford professor, forced the Coronation ring on to the wrong finger, causing the Queen great pain. There was an interval in the proceedings, while the Queen retired to St. Edward's chapel. Here Lord Melbourne made her laugh by saying it was less like a chapel than anything he had ever seen—pointing to the sandwiches and drinks which were spread out on the altar. The Queen was somewhat burdened by the weight of the crown, sceptre and orb and she described herself as " loaded." Some people said that she was in tears with the pain of her ring and the encumbrance of the symbols of sovereignty as she drove back to the palace, but this was not so; she heard the barking of her favourite spaniel as the coach turned into the courtyard and she said to the Duchess of Sutherland, " There— that's Dash." She was delighted when, after dinner, Lord Melbourne said to her with tears in his eyes, " You did it beautifully—every part of it, with so much taste." And speaking of taste—meaning the natural grace with which she had behaved— he added that that was " a thing that you can't give a person advice upon: it must be left to a person."

At this period the Queen was universally popular, for the spectacle of a young girl discharging the historic duties of the English monarchy was calculated to warm the hearts of her subjects. Those early years of her reign were romantic and at a time when people, encouraged by the novels of Sir Walter Scott, were looking backwards to the age of chivalry they saw the Queen as possessing something of the mystic grace of Queen Guinevere—a being to whom men were proud to offer their lance or their heart. Romantic early Victorians conceived that they had hopeless passions for the Queen; Dickens, then a young writer winning his first triumphs, imagined himself head over ears in love with the Queen and, in a letter to a friend, he wrote the feeble if expressive ditty:

> " *My heart is at Windsor*
> *My heart is not here:*
> *My heart is at Windsor*
> *A following my dear.*"

More serious was the conduct of half crazy gentlemen who tried to get into conversation with her when she was riding in the Park, or shouted into her carriage. Once one of these amiable maniacs forced his way into the Chapel Royal and, standing in front of the pew where the Queen was, began to bow and kiss his hand to her. As he was led away by chapel officials, he called out, " Your Majesty, I am being arrested in church." He added in tones of shocked reproof " Queen Victoria."

Yet triumphantly successful as had been the

opening months of Queen Victoria's reign, her popularity was in one respect vulnerable—that was over politics. She was completely identified with a single political party—the Whigs. Her Ministers were naturally all of that persuasion, her courtiers and ladies were all drawn from Whig families and, what was more serious, she never invited Tories or Conservatives to anything except purely formal parties from which it was impossible to exclude them. To the Whigs she gave complete confidence. Nor will it be overlooked that loyalty was ever a predominant quality of the Queen: if she trusted people, she trusted them completely and wished the world to know it. But the issue was complicated by the strength of the Tory Party: they had greatly improved their position in the General Election of 1837—for in those days an election always had to be held after the accession of a new sovereign. In fact the Whigs, who had been in office (with one small break of a few months) since 1830, were tottering and the Tories were eager to give them that extra push which might hurl them from office. This happened in the early summer of 1839; the Whig Government was defeated, and the Queen was faced with the horrible prospect of losing " dear, good Lord Melbourne " and having to accept Sir Robert Peel—an able statesman but solemn and uncouth—as her Prime Minister.

From this unwelcome change from Whiggery to

Toryism the Queen was saved by what is called The Bedchamber Plot. This curious, amusing but intricate question is too often slurred over in history books: it is very revealing of the Queen's character.

The Queen's Ladies consisted of a Mistress of the Robes, ladies-in-waiting and women of the bed-chamber. They were all members of the aristocracy (though the ladies-in-waiting were of higher rank than the women of the bedchamber) and they each had spells throughout the year when they were in waiting. When the Queen came to the throne Melbourne (perhaps mistakenly) had appointed ladies sympathetic to the Whig party. He allowed no Tories at all. The Queen had rather naturally become devoted to them: indeed they were the people on whom she relied for those private parties and dances which she so greatly enjoyed, and were in fact her bosom friends. In those days it was customary for a king to appoint members of the household whose politics agreed with those of the Government in power, but it had not been usual for his wife, the queen, to change her ladies with each change of Government. In an interview with Sir Robert Peel the Queen pointed this out but Sir Robert replied " Your Majesty is a Queen Regnant." He was trying to explain that her position as Queen in her own right was different from that of a Queen Consort, who merely derived her title from being the wife of the reigning sovereign.

The Queen was furious and in describing her talks with Peel she said, with a truly Elizabethan ring, " The Queen of England will not submit to such trickery." There was perhaps a genuine misunderstanding between Peel and the Queen; she thought he meant to change all her ladies, whereas he seems to have meant that she should only change some. But Peel refused to form a government without a change of some kind. This the Queen refused to do and Peel abandoned his efforts to form a government, so that, after all, the Queen was able to continue with her beloved Whigs as the Government. She wrote to Melbourne that she rejoiced at having got out of the hand of people who would have sacrificed the Queen's feelings " to their bad party purposes."

A consequence of these events was that the Queen became intensely unpopular with the Conservative aristocracy. The first sign of this was when she drove in the customary carriage procession from Windsor Castle to Ascot races, in 1839 after the Bedchamber Crisis. As the Queen drove by one of the stands, some titled ladies were distinctly heard to hiss. The leader of these excitable peeresses was the Conservative Duchess of Montrose—who ran a racing stable under the pseudonym of " Mr. Manton," and many years later electrified Victorian society by marrying a gentleman forty-six years younger than herself. But far more serious were the open attacks made on the Queen by Conservative speakers in the country. In the respectable, cathedral city of Canterbury the Conservative member launched a fierce attack on the Queen. He began with a broadside against her uncle Leopold whom he called " the citizen King of the Belgians " and " the serf of France." He continued that no one could regret more than he did " the growing unpopularity of the Queen." He linked her name with that of King James II and said that " the people of England would never consent that the Crown should be degraded and debased for the inglorious ease " of the Queen. His speech was punctuated, as the reporter observed, with " tremendous cheers." In the North of England a Conservative speaker said:

" When anyone aimed a blow at this epicene administration, down they skulked behind the embroidered petticoats and the flounces and furbelows of the ladies of the Court." (Epicene was a well-chosen word meaning " common to both sexes.") Sixty years afterwards when the Queen was discussing these turbulent days with a friend she said " I was very young then, and perhaps I should act differently if it was all to be done again." Yet that is open to doubt for throughout this crisis the Queen showed two qualities which were the very foundation stone of her character. She had strong feminine partialities and in defence of them she showed a degree of inflexibility or of obstinacy which was dangerous. At the same time she stood up to both Peel and Wellington over this issue with a courage which was admirable.

Certainly the Queen had triumphed by having her own way, but she had only done this by jeopardising her popularity and by running a really serious risk. Watching these matters from afar, her uncle decided that the time had come for the Queen to marry, and that she needed the counsel and comfort of a husband.

The question of the Queen's marriage had naturally caused both speculation and gossip ever since she came to the throne. A queen without a husband had been unknown to English history since the days of Queen Elizabeth and it was not forgotten that the suitors and projected marriages of that illustrious Tudor kept all Europe on tenterhooks. That Queen's caution and her decision to choose the blessed independence of spinsterhood are some indication of the perils of a bad choice—of the danger both to personal happiness and the welfare of England which might result from introducing a prince of unsound character or one eager to play an active political part. Although nearly three centuries divided Queen Elizabeth from Queen Victoria the dangers which might have arisen through an ill-judged marriage were undiminished. The possibility that the Queen should marry an Englishman does not seem to have been considered.

All Roman Catholics were excluded unless they were prepared to change their religion. Reigning European sovereigns or their heirs were likewise barred, because it would have created impossible problems if two countries—say Holland and England—had had the same monarch. Consequently the choice was not wide. In fact the only names seriously canvassed were those of the Queen's cousins. On her father's side the only possible choice was Prince George of Cambridge—a bluff, ugly prince whose massive statue stands in the middle of Whitehall. When the Queen in fact became engaged she saw Prince George and remarked that he seemed " happy to be *clear* of me." He showed his happiness by marrying a beautiful actress a few weeks afterwards.

On her mother's side the Queen had a number of possible cousins, including Prince Albert, son of the reigning Duke of Saxe-Coburg, who was very strongly favoured by King Leopold. It was arranged that he, accompanied by his elder brother, should pay a visit to Windsor in the autumn of 1839. The two cousins had met in earlier days but matters did not look exactly promising. To her uncle, the Queen wrote, " I *may* like him as a friend, and as a *cousin*, and as a *brother*, but not *more*." On his side the Prince wrote to a friend " Victoria is said to be incredibly stubborn. . . . She delights in court ceremonies, etiquette and trivial formalities. She is said to take not the slightest interest in nature, to enjoy sitting up at night and sleeping late into the day." This was by no means inaccurate, for the Queen was in no hurry to give up her gay and independent life in exchange for the control of a husband and the ties of a nursery. However the Prince, who was a few months younger than she, was exceptionally handsome, agreeable and, as she wrote at once to her uncle, " fascinating." Three days after Prince Albert arrived, Lord Melbourne, who was staying at Windsor, wrote confidentially to a member of the Cabinet, saying in his amusing way, " The mind is, in fact, made up." One of the most curious and peculiar attributes of a female sovereign is that she must propose to her husband—thereby reversing the natural order. At midday one morning she sent for the Prince and asked him to marry her. He accepted. The matter was kept a profound secret and although the Queen danced much with her lover at informal balls in the castle, even the ladies of the Court were ignorant of what had been arranged. To one of her intimates the Queen wrote, " We have been very gay here and I have become a great galloper." Only Lord Melbourne, King Leopold and probably Lehzen knew what had been arranged. Six weeks later the Queen told her mother and her uncles and aunts, and called a meeting of the Privy Council at Buckingham Palace. The meeting was a brilliant one—all the privy councillors attending in naval or military uniform or in Court dress and in the case of the lawyers in full judicial robes. Trembling and blushing, but with a clear voice, the Queen read her speech referring to her marriage as "a matter which deeply concerns the welfare of my people, and the happiness of my future life." Her old aunt, the Duchess of Gloucester, said that she must have found it very embarrassing to talk about her marriage before so many gentlemen. She replied that it was not so bad as having herself to propose to the Prince. They were married in the Chapel Royal in St. James's Palace on February 10th, 1840. On the following day the Queen wrote to her uncle, " He is an Angel."

* 3 *

Years of Happiness

FOR THE next twenty years the life of the Queen, although it was full and active, was blissfully happy. This is explained by the fact that she had married a man who was not only clever and handsome but completely unselfish. In one important respect she gave way to him at once, and this quickly changed her whole manner of life. This was over her love for London. She had hated to be away from Buckingham Palace, loved parties, balls, plays and operas, enjoyed the tittle-tattle about her friends and tended to be put out and bored in the country. Prince Albert was just the opposite. He danced beautifully but did not enjoy it, parties and indeed all the conventional entertainments of the English aristocracy left him cold: he hated late hours and like his mother-in-law, the Duchess of Kent, was apt to nod with sleep after dinner. He revelled in the country and in the study of natural things. Within six months of her marriage the Queen was, in this respect, transformed and began to prefer the peace and quiet of the country. She, who did not even know the difference between an oak and an elm when she became Queen, started to notice such matters and surprised one of the ladies of the Court, when they were out walking together by pointing to a tree and saying, "That is a tulip tree, you see—a rare tree, but yet hardy."

She found that Windsor Castle, with its gardens far removed from the part she lived in, was too formal. Since it belonged to the Crown and was not the private property of the Sovereign, they could make no substantial alterations and improvements there without leave from the Government. In this connection, the Queen once said that the Government was the bane of her life. Accordingly they decided to purchase, for their own personal possession, a small estate in the Isle of Wight called Osborne. They generally spent as much of the spring and summer here as they possibly could—a decision which was not popular with Cabinet Ministers and others, having official business with the Crown, who rather groaned at having to make the sea crossing from Southampton to the island. The Prince toiled manfully in the garden, while the Queen sat under the trees working on official business or keeping her journal up to date. But the Prince had been nurtured in the mountains of Southern Germany, and he found the flat ground

QUEEN VICTORIA AND PRINCE ALBERT
Photographed by Roger Fenton in 1854

of the Thames valley, round Windsor, very ener-
vating and depressing, and even Osborne did not
quite afford him the champagne-air of mountains.
He persuaded the Queen to spend a summer
holiday in the mountains of Scotland, and from
their immediate enjoyment of the clear air and
splendid scenery may be dated their decision to
make a third home for themselves at Balmoral.
Both of them delighted in the natural courtesy and
dignity of the Highlander and they loved the care-
free life in which they could call on the cottagers in
their own homes without state or formality. On
their side the Highlanders were naturally proud
that the Queen should have come to live in Scotland.
On one occasion the Queen said to a young gillie,
" It must be very dull after we have gone."

He replied, " It's just like death come all at
once."

Perhaps most of all, the Queen enjoyed the opportunity of travelling *incognito* in the Highlands. On
one occasion she and the Prince rode on ponies—
part of the way posting in a carriage—to a village
many miles north of Balmoral where they stayed in
an inn. They called themselves Lord and Lady
Churchill, while the real Lady Churchill who, as
Lady-in-Waiting, was with them called herself
Miss Spencer and the Prince's private secretary,
General Grey, called himself Dr. Grey. Like King
Louis XVI on the flight to Varennes or like King

Henry V before Agincourt the Queen experienced the curious thrill (reserved for illustrious persons) of not being recognised—although Brown, her personal Highland servant, very nearly gave everything away by addressing her as " Your Majesty " when helping her out of the carriage.

The lack of privacy in ordinary life was undoubtedly the heaviest part of the burden of sovereignty for the Queen. Only seldom was it possible for her to be alone with her husband. In the evening there were almost always guests to dinner including all the ladies and gentlemen who were in waiting. After dinner there was general conversation or a circle was formed and the Queen moved round the room making conversation with each individual. This lack of privacy was the explanation why she once wrote to her uncle of " my *much* disliked position." Again there was always the possibility that a serious political crisis would develop at a time when the Queen was responsible for the care of an infant. (She had nine children to look after.) This is the explanation why she once wrote to her uncle:

" I am every day more convinced that *we women*, if we *are* to be good women, *feminine* and *amiable* and *domestic*, are *not fitted to reign*; at least it is *contre gré* (against their will) that they drive themselves to the *work* which it entails." The Queen, as will be noticed, had a ready command of the French idiom.

For someone in her position it was very difficult to do anything spontaneously, the consequences of everything she did—even the remote contingencies— had to be carefully pondered. Could she, for example, go and see a play in Lent or would there be an outcry from the clergy? She had to get the permission of her Prime Minister before she could go. Of all her subjects she was, in many respects, the least free. But the Prince by sharing her difficulties and problems with good humour made her life, as she once expressed it, " bright and happy." The following is a good illustration of this. In 1845 the Queen and Prince paid a visit to Germany: she was greatly distressed because it was reported in the German newspapers that she looked cross and disagreeable. She said to the Prince that if she had looked cross, it was only because she was shy and also tired after a long journey and she asked rather pathetically " What *am* I to do another time? " " Oh, this," he said, springing up and giving a wonderful imitation of a ballet dancer's pirouette, accompanied by a grin from ear to ear. The Queen's distress was dissolved in laughter.

The broad picture of the Royal Family during these twenty happy years is of a charming, united and care-free family. The public anxieties and preoccupations of the parents were not allowed to interfere with the happiness of the children. On New Year's morning the young princes and princesses would gather outside their mother and father's bedroom and shout in unison " *Prosit Neu Jahr.*" Each family birthday was marked by a little ceremony in a room, beautifully decorated, in which the person whose birthday was celebrated was led to a table piled high with presents. On Christmas Eve they all gathered round a tree blazing with lights and loaded with presents. One of the Queen's daughters, on entering the room, was heard to say, " Really it is a trifle too extravagant." Later on the same day one of the youthful Princes was noticed firing off his pop-gun at the calf of his father's leg. In those days the Court Circular— which is the official record of the doings of the Sovereign and the Royal Family during the day— was far more detailed than is possible in the twentieth century. This is an extract from the Court Circular in 1855 when the eldest of the royal children was fifteen and the youngest who is mentioned was five. The Court was at Windsor.

" The Queen and the Prince, accompanied by the Prince of Wales and Prince Alfred, walked in the Home Park this morning. The Princess Royal and the Princess Alice rode in the Riding House. The Princesses Helena and Louise and Prince Arthur took a drive in an open carriage and four." The Court Circular almost invariably ended with a list of the guests staying to dinner at the castle with the name of the Regimental Band which played during dinner, and the announcement that the Queen's private band played afterwards.

There were of course the natural disasters of family life which the Queen, being warm-hearted, felt acutely. Perhaps one of the worst of these was when Eos, the Prince's favourite greyhound which he had brought with him from Germany, was shot through the lung by a visiting Prince at a pheasant shoot at Windsor. The Queen, with typical frankness, confessed that it made her quite ill, and she wrote to her uncle describing how the dog " walked about wrapped up in flannel." The greyhound fortunately got well. It is only necessary to contrast the Queen in earlier times at Kensington Palace with the Queen after her marriage to realise the transformation in her life which had been effected by her happiness. When the Prince of Orange came to visit her after her marriage she said that he hardly recognised her—she was so cheerful and free—compared with the time he had previously seen her at Kensington Palace, when she was oppressed and kept down. After she had been married three years she wrote to her uncle, " Indeed, dearest uncle, I will venture to say that not only no Royal Menage is to be found equal to *ours*, but no other *ménage* is to be compared to ours, nor is *any one* to be compared, take him altogether, to my *dearest Angel* ! " Exaggerated language, some may feel, but in reality not far from the truth. For she came to rely entirely on the judgment and point of view of the Prince, grudging every moment that she was separated from him and needing no other companion than him. She never learned to make confidants and companions of her children and even when they grew up she was never completely at ease in their company—a great misfortune in the circumstances of her later life.

Together the Queen and Prince conducted the Court and official life of the Monarchy with a brilliance which has never been surpassed. The English nation was climbing towards the peak of commercial prosperity and the aristocracy, at that time, was proud and exclusive. A Court Ball, a presentation party or a levée was in consequence a gathering of great splendour and dignity. King Leopold, who was familiar with all the other European courts, noticed this and observed of the English Court, " There is hardly a country where such magnificence exists." He went on to say that although Austria had wealth and tradition " the Court was not elegant from its nature." This was a polite way of saying that the Emperor at that time was unfortunately an imbecile. The Queen was not a regal figure in the sense that she was not imposing, but she had that kind of dignity which comes from knowing exactly what to do. On one occasion she was visiting a foreign royalty and they went to the opera. On entering the box first the hostess hung back uncertain what to do. The Queen, with that effortless gliding which was familiar to all who studied her movements, moved quickly and decidedly right to the front of the box and bowed repeatedly to the assembled company. Perhaps one of the most splendid entertainments was in 1842 when the Queen gave a fancy-dress ball or *Bal costumé*, as it was called in the elegant language of those times. The Queen was dressed as Queen Philippa and the Prince as Edward III. This affair gave great offence in Paris because the King of France of those far-away days was represented at the Ball and did homage to King Edward.

The formal entertaining of foreign royalty was a frequent event during the Queen's married life. In a single year (1844) she entertained the Emperor of Russia, the King of the French and the King of Saxony. The King of the French was invested with the Garter but it was not thought quite seemly that the Queen should fix a garter on to a gentleman's leg so the Prince did it, leaving the Queen to pull the strap tight. Although neither the Queen nor the Prince approved of the way in which Napoleon III had seized power, they entertained him at Windsor and were fascinated by him and the Empress Eugénie and went to visit them in Paris the following year. They took the Prince of Wales who was thirteen and as they were leaving he went up to the Emperor and asked if he might remain with him in Paris. The Emperor replied, " I think your mother and father might miss you." " Oh no "—came the answer—" there are plenty more of us at home." Perhaps the highlight of this visit to France was when the Emperor and Queen went to the tomb of the great Napoleon. In her journal the Queen described this event in prose which was vivid and simple, characteristic of all her writings:

" There I stood, at the arm of Napoleon III, his nephew, before the coffin of England's bitterest foe: I, the granddaughter of that King who hated him most, and who most vigorously opposed him, and this very nephew, who bears his name, being my nearest and dearest ally. The organ of the church was playing ' God Save The Queen ' at the time and this solemn scene took place by torchlight, and during a thunderstorm, strange and wonderful indeed. It seems, as if in this tribute of respect to a departed and dead foe, old enmities and rivalries were wiped out, and the seal of Heaven placed upon that bond of unity, which is now happily established between two great and powerful nations. May Heaven bless and prosper it." And of this visit a Marshal of France could say with truth that not even Napoleon, entering Paris in all the glory of one of his victories, could draw the populace and their cheers as did *La Reine d' Angleterre*.

The Queen's sense of humour was never very far from the surface and there was always a risk at these ceremonies that she night break into laughter. There was an occasion when a French girl, who was presenting the Queen with a bouquet, forgot her words in the middle of her speech. " *Ah mon Dieu* " she said looking up at the Queen in agony. The Queen tried to help her by taking the bouquet and starting to thank her but the girl said " *Attendez! Je vais me rappeler.*" Both Queen and Emperor shook with suppressed laughter, but managed to keep their gravity. The Queen's relations with foreign rulers were on occasion less formal, The envoy of the Iman of Muscat—a principality on the Tropic of Cancer, close to the Arabian Sea— announced to the British Foreign Secretary that he had brought with him some presents for the Queen with a letter from the Iman. The Queen was highly delighted with the letter which ran thus: " List of Articles sent for Her Most Gracious Majesty, The Mighty Queen, a trifling Gift scarce worth being mentioned.

Two Pearl Necklaces

Two Emeralds

An Ornament made like a Crown

Ten cashmere shawls

One box containing four Bottles Otto of Roses

Four horses, before mentioned in a former letter, but for the transmission of which no opportunity offered in Bombay, but now sent in my own ship.

Through your kindness have those things taken from Ali bin Nassur, and make an excuse for me to Her Most Gracious Majesty, and peace be on you."

But it was not only on ceremonial occasions and in dealings with fellow-sovereigns that the Queen showed that she was happy, and enjoyed her life in spite of its work and burdens. She had, for example, a rather unexpected taste for the sea: the Prince tended to be seasick and liked it less. Soon after her accession she went down to Woolwich where some of her Coburg relatives were embarking for the Continent. When she came up from their cabins to leave the ship, the officers crowded round eager to help her down the side of the ship, but she said in her clear, decisive voice, " No help, thank you. I am used to this." Then she said to one of her ladies, " I was quite glad to find myself in a ship again—the first time since I came to the throne. I do like ships." In 1842, when she was staying at Brighton in The Pavilion, that lovely but fantastic building put up by her uncle George IV, she went to a naval review at Portsmouth and was enormously impressed by *The Queen*—a wooden ship with a crew of almost a thousand men. Queen Victoria was struck by her width and roominess, and on going round the ship she gave general pleasure by tasting the grog and soup. In describing this venture she wrote:

" It was a great pleasure for the Queen to be at

sea again, and not a creature *thought* even of being sick. . . . I think it is in these immense wooden walls that our real greatness exists, and I am proud to think that no *other* nation can *equal* us in this." While the royal yacht (the *Victoria and Albert*) was largely used to provide a shuttle service between Southampton and the Isle of Wight in the later part of her reign, she used it for much longer expeditions—for example to Ireland and up to Scotland—in these early days. In spite of her boast about seasickness she disliked dirty weather at sea and although the following story is possibly apocryphal it illustrates her character. When crossing to Ireland the yacht ran into a rough sea and was buffeted by an enormous wave. The Queen immediately sent for the captain and said, " It must not happen again."

Possibly the finest and most potent spectacle afforded by the English monarchy is the sight of the sovereign, accompanied by members of the Royal House, leading generals and foreign *aides de camp* at a large military review. For a woman this is a singularly exacting task and, on the advice of the Duke of Wellington, the Queen did not hold a review on horseback in the early days of her reign. She had not ridden for two years before coming to the throne and anything in the way of a fall would have been a formidable blow to her dignity. By degrees she gained confidence and in 1842 she took part in a brilliant review at Wormwood Scrubbs— that fine open space to the west of London made familiar to most people by the Victorian prison which adorns its western extremity. She drove from Buckingham Palace in an open landau and then was greeted under a railway bridge at the edge of the Scrubbs by the Duke of Wellington. In the comparative privacy of the bridge she mounted a light chestnut Arab charger, which had been previously led there from the royal stables. The general impression of the review, heightened by dazzling June sunshine, was one of great splendour. The Queen wore the Windsor uniform—a blue riding-habit with crimson facings, and a black round hat with a black lace veil. She was wearing across from her left shoulder the blue riband of the Garter. She was immediately followed by the Prince and the leading generals of the British Army. She then rode down the lines of the two regiments of Life Guards and the 8th Royal Hussars, delighting the soldiers by raising her whip in salute as she passed the Colours. There was always the risk on these occasions that some sudden movement by the soldiers or an unexpected cheer from the crowd would disturb the equanimity of the Queen's horse —an eventuality which always made the Duke of Wellington rather touchy at these Reviews, but all passed off perfectly and the Queen wrote to her uncle, " I rode on my little Barb at a review of

Cavalry at Wormwood Scrubbs on Saturday, *dont je suis bien fière.*"

Unhappily the Queen had ample reason for showing some nervousness in public during these early years of her reign. Just as young men had made it fashionable to pretend that they were in love with her before her marriage, another and more seedy type of youth now made it fashionable to attempt to murder her. The first attempt was in the summer after her marriage when a youth named Edward Oxford fired at her. She and the Prince were driving out from Buckingham Palace in a low carriage, and they turned up Constitution Hill, Oxford was standing, with arms folded, on the path at the bottom of the Green Park. As the carriage drew level, he fired. The Prince rose in the carriage as if to jump out and seize Oxford, when he saw that Oxford had drawn a second pistol. Prince Albert attempted to shield the Queen who wisely ducked her head and the bullet whizzed harmlessly above her. The Government naturally thought that the assailant might belong to some gang of desperadoes or even political fanatics, but careful examination showed that Oxford, a pot-boy in a public house, was of imbecile tendencies and had no experience of fire-arms except that which he had gained on the previous afternoon at a species of primitive fun-fair in the Strand. The next attempt was exactly two years later when a young man called Francis shot at her—again on Constitution Hill. He was standing on the opposite side of the carriage-way from Oxford. He fired at such close range that he blackened the face of the equerry who was riding by the wheel of the carriage. The crime was clearly planned and there was no suggestion, as in Oxford's case, of imbecility. Francis was condemned to death but, by the leniency of the Queen, he was transported to Australia instead of being hanged. The most disagreeable, though not the most dangerous, experience of the Queen was when a crazy Army officer struck her on the temple, with a cane, as she was getting out of her carriage in Piccadilly. Although the newspapers tried to make out that the Queen only drove out in fear and trembling after these attempts on her life she bore them in fact with the greatest fortitude. On the evening after she had been struck in Piccadilly, she was due to go to the opera. Her lady-in-waiting begged her not to go on the grounds that she was hurt. The reply was worthy of Queen Elizabeth, " I shall certainly go—so as to show them how little I mind."

But the eccentricity of the Queen's subjects was not always manifested against her in malevolence or hostility. In 1852 there died a notorious miser called John Camden Neild. This gentleman—an old Etonian and a member of Cambridge University —had been a barrister. Towards the end of his life he lived in a large house—No. 5 Cheyne Walk, Chelsea. This was sparsely furnished and he had latterly slept on the floor. He always dressed in dirty clothing which he refused to have brushed because the bristles of the clothes brush might damage the nap of his coat. He said that he could not afford an overcoat and his only protection against the weather was a huge green umbrella. He owned considerable property in Kent and Buckinghamshire. When repairs had to be done to the roof of a property he owned, he spent the day on the roof to make certain that the workmen did not waste a moment of the time for which he was paying. He lived chiefly on eggs which he bought cheap off his tenants. When he died he left very nearly half a million and when his will was opened it was found that he had left the whole of this vast fortune to the Queen " begging Her Majesty's most gracious acceptance of it for her sole use and benefit." After considerable hesitation the Queen decided to accept it, first giving handsome legacies to all who had looked after Mr. Neild and to his executors. With characteristic nineteenth-century piety she put up a reredos and stained glass window to his memory in the church in Buckinghamshire where he lies buried.

But any estimate of the Queen's life during her twenty years of marriage would be incomplete which did not show her debt to the Prince Consort in the conduct of politics and of the relations between the Crown and the Government. The happiness of her private life with the Prince and her children, and the zest and gaiety of her public appearances were in a sense secondary to the real business of her life—the task of dealing with the piles of official papers which were daily laid before her to approve or sign. But inevitably her private happiness eased the burden of her public duties. This King Leopold had been quick to see for he wrote to the Queen, as soon as he heard of her engagement, " In your position which may and will, perhaps, become in future even more difficult in a political point of view, *you could not exist* without having a *happy and agreeable interieur* (home life)." This was singularly shrewd since the politics of the twenty years from 1840 to 1860 were to prove very difficult and complex. At home the passing of the Reform Bill in 1832 meant that the long-fought battle between Whigs and Tories had ended. From now onwards the Whigs were gradually to yield ground to the new forces of Liberalism pressing for all kinds of social and economic changes. The Tory Party, after giving way over the issue of Free Trade in 1845, became less the party of the country gentlemen, less the exponents of the old slogan " Church and State " and more the party of stability. But these great changes meant that parties in the House of Commons were weaker and Governments

came and went during these years with bewildering
speed—a Government might fall because the Pro-
tectionist wing of the Tories deserted them in a
critical division or because the Liberals and Radicals
decided to abandon their Whig allies. On at least
two occasions in these twenty years the country was
left without a government. When Sir Robert Peel
resigned on the issue of Free Trade in 1845 it proved
impossible to find a successor from his political
opponents and he was obliged to carry on with a
fast melting majority in the House of Commons.
This was the occasion of one of *Punch's* best cartoons.
The Queen was depicted as the mistress of a house
interviewing a buttons boy (Lord John Russell)
with a view to employment. (He was a diminutive
man and having been twice married, each time to
a widow, he was jocularly known as The Widow's
Mite. Consequently he did not look amiss in the
cartoon as a page boy.) The Queen is saying to the
boy " But I am afraid, John, that you are not
strong enough for the place." This proved correct.

In 1846 Russell formed a Government which
lasted for five years. When he fell in February
1851 there was such confusion that the country
was without a Government for some days. *Punch*
commented " Everybody went to call upon everybody. The hall porters were never known to have
had such a time of it, but though knocking at
doors continued throughout the whole day, nothing

seemed to answer." This weakness of parties in the House of Commons and the uncertainty which it caused gave the Queen great anxiety because it meant that instead of there being an obvious alternative Government she had to interview a number of statesmen before a strong Cabinet could be formed. All this tended to increase the political power of the Crown. Side by side with these events at home went the emergence of of strong Liberal feeling on the Continent. The old monarchies, established after the overthrow of Napoleon were all struggling by the end of the 1840's to smother popular movements. France, Italy, Germany, the Peninsular all had the same tale to tell: only the vast empire of the Tsars seemed safe from popular disturbance. The part to be played by England in these agitated politics of Europe was a matter of great controversy. Palmerston, who was foreign secretary or Prime Minister for many of these years, was strongly in favour of supporting all popular or left wing movements on the Continent: the Queen and Prince, who had many friends and relations among the rulers of Europe, sponsored a more moderate policy and, in particular, the point of view that England should not fan the flames of Liberal feeling in those countries where, without such encouragement, Liberal opinions would have been unlikely to make themselves felt.

The influence of the Prince in politics was profound, but it was naturally done through the Queen
and his first task was to develop her reliance on
herself and to give her confidence. Her trust in the
Whigs and Lord Melbourne had been so complete
that she had really never questioned him or his
leading ministers but had agreed with all they asked
her to do. She had not carefully examined each
measure proposed but had accepted it without
necessarily fully understanding it. In the early days
of her marriage a paper came in from the Government marked " Sign immediately." The Prince
thought it disgraceful that the Government should
treat the Queen with this lack of respect, and
urged her to hold it up for twenty-four hours. This
she refused to do. But with the fall of Melbourne
everything became easier and, tutored by the
Prince, the Queen examined all papers with the
greatest care and had the benefit of the Prince's
advice in disputing any point with the Government
or objecting to any particular line of policy. This
active intervention by the Queen first became
marked in her relations with Palmerston. The
machinery for conducting the foreign policy of the
country is done to-day by a series of telegrams from
the Foreign Office to the various British ambassadors
abroad. In Palmerston's day it was done by
despatches sent by special messenger or courier.
The Queen expected to see and approve all impor-

tant despatches before they were sent. Palmerston, faced by great pressure of business, frequently turned a blind eye to the Queen's wishes, often sending off the despatches before she had seen them and sometimes making considerable changes after she had seen and approved them. Palmerston was Foreign Secretary from 1846 to the end of 1851 and throughout those years the friction between the Court and the Foreign Office was serious. Writing to the Prime Minister, who was Lord John Russell, on behalf of the Queen, the Prince went so far as to say that they really felt they could not go on with Palmerston and in conversation the Queen said to the Prime Minister:

" I have no confidence in Lord Palmerston: I feel very uneasy from one day to another as to what may happen: I am afraid that some day I shall have to tell you that I cannot put up with Lord Palmerston, which might be very disagreeable and awkward." While the Sovereign has an unquestioned right to dismiss a minister (which was what the Queen was politely telling Lord John) such a right had not been exercised for many years.

For a time things went more smoothly until the extraordinary episode connected with General Haynau. This gentleman—an Austrian commander —had become very unpopular in England because of the severity with which he had put down a rising in Hungary and, in particular, for having thrashed some women accomplices of the Hungarian rebels. In the autumn of 1850 he was staying in England, and decided to pay a visit to the brewery of Barclay Perkins—which had once belonged to Dr. Johnson's friends the Thrales and which was situated at Bankside on the river opposite St. Paul's Cathedral. Within two minutes of his arrival at the brewery the identity of their illustrious visitor spread among the labourers and draymen. Collecting brooms they swept up the horse dung, which abounded, and began to pelt the unhappy Austrian with these agreeable pellets, shouting at the tops of their voices, "Down with the Austrian Butcher," and with the quick wit of the Londoner the cries were varied by "Down with General Hyena." The poor Austrian, who was by this time thoroughly frightened, fled into the street—pursued by a motley army of workers who belaboured him with shovels and were said to have dragged him through the gutter by his moustache of which he had an exceptionally fine specimen. He managed to escape and dashed into The George Inn—a ramshackle building of the seventeenth century—and frightened the ancient landlady by tearing upstairs and locking himself into the first bedroom he saw. Here he was rescued by the police.

The episode—though perhaps disgraceful—was spirited and English. Plainly, however, the circumstances demanded an abject apology to the Austrian

Government. Palmerston managed to send this apology, without first showing it to the Queen, and also managed to slip in a rather insulting allusion to the reactionary policy of the Austrian Government. The Queen sharply remonstrated with Palmerston but he tried to soothe her with a letter of characteristic flippancy. He started by regretting the mistake which the General had made in not shaving off his long moustachios which made him a figure easy to identify and difficult to forget. He spoke of him as a great moral criminal and explained to the Queen that the public looked on the General with much the same feelings as they exhibited towards Mrs. Manning. This lady had recently been tried for murder and found guilty. Her execution—which in those days was public— roused the crowd to a frenzy of indignation against her—so much so that Dickens wrote a letter to *The Times* complaining of the callousness of the English mob. (She was the original of Lady Dedlock's maid in Dickens's novel *Bleak House*.) The fact that she walked to the scaffold dressed in black satin made that material unfashionable for many years. The comparison of the General with this murderess may have been effective but it was highly offensive to the Queen. A year after the episode with General Haynau, Palmerston, without consulting either his Cabinet colleagues or the Queen, approved the conduct of Napoleon III in

overthrowing the Republic of France and seizing
power. This was too much, and the Queen persuaded the Prime Minister to ask for his resignation
which took place on December 16th.

The story of the struggle between the Queen and
Palmerston is of considerable interest to all who
seek to understand her character. She had travelled
far and developed much since those days of " good
Lord Melbourne's " government when, so far as
politics were concerned, she did what she was told,
merely agreeing with everything that was brought
before her. She made it abundantly clear that she
had a point of view, and that it was one which
could not just be trampled underfoot. But she was
much more than an obstructionist. Under the
tuition of the Prince she felt strongly that the
conduct of foreign policy should not be slap-dash
and governed by expediency but that morality and
principle should be the foundations on which policy
should rest. To Palmerston this was incomprehensible: he felt that England should take advantage
of any opportunity to further the cause of freedom
in Europe. The Queen did not object to this in
principle: what she disliked was Palmerston's
anxiety to stir up trouble for other European
governments and the general dislike of England
which this policy produced. She wrote to Lord
John to complain that Palmerston had received an
address from English radicals in which friendly

rulers had been alluded to as Despots and Assassins. The outlook between the two was antipathetic. In conversation and in letters to her uncle she always called him Pilgerstein—being the German for a palmer or pedlar. She once wrote of him as " the old sinner." Palmerston's policy was extremely vigorous and successful, but that should not blind us to the risks he ran and we certainly cannot blame the Queen for becoming conscious of danger and for trying to overcome it.

A few years later, at the height of the war between England and Russia in the Crimea, Palmerston became Prime Minister and it is greatly to the credit both of him and of the Queen that the old animosities were buried. In her journal the Queen wrote that his appointment was " not personally agreeable to me, but I think of nothing but the country." At the end of the war she offered him the Garter to mark her sense of the way in which he had upheld " the honour and interests of the country." In a graceful reply Palmerston said that his heavy task had been " rendered comparatively easy by the enlightened views which your Majesty has taken of all the great affairs in which your Majesty's Empire has been engaged."

It was during these years that the first signs appeared of the spell which the subtle genius of Disraeli was to weave over the mind of the Queen. The Leader of the House of Commons had then to write accounts of the day's proceedings for the private information of the sovereign. The majority of Victorian statesmen managed to make these reports singularly dull and repetitive. Not so Disraeli. Referring to one of his rival Gladstone's speeches he writes:

" It was not a happy effort, and the debate, for a while revived by his interposition, continued to languish until this hour (nine o'clock), with successive relays of mediocrity, until it yielded its last gasp in the arms of Mr. Slaney." On a subsequent occasion he wrote:

" The night tranquil and interesting—Lord Bury, with much intelligence, introduced the subject of the Straits Settlements; the speech of Sir J. Elphinstone, master of the subject and full of striking details, produced a great effect. His vindication of the convict population of Singapore, as the moral element of that strange society, might have been considered the richest humour, had it not been for its unmistakeable sincerity. His enquiry of the Governor's lady, who never hired any servant but a convict, whether she employed in her nursery ' Thieves or Murderers' and the answer ' Always Murderers ' was very effective." He explained to the Queen that his letters " were merely rough notes, written on the field of battle " to make something different from the ordinary newspaper reports. That the Queen appreciated this correspondence is clear from a letter to her uncle in which she writes, " Mr. Disraeli (*alias* Dizzy) writes very curious reports to me of the House of Commons proceedings—much in the style of his books."

But throughout these twenty years one other characteristic of the Queen becomes apparent and deserves to be emphasised. She had an intense, a burning love for her country. Although she was no doubt tiresome, on occasions, to her Ministers she was throughout inspired by the one feeling of what was best for the country. In the alarms and despairing moments of the Crimean war she was always resolute, anxious for the well-being of her soldiers but confident that the honour of the country was safe in their hands. Her powers of description, which put to shame the talents of many a journalist, were always used to the best advantage in describing anything to do with the Army. Could there be a simpler yet more moving account of the glory and pathos of troops leaving for the front than this extract from one of her letters?

" The last battalion of the Guards embarked to-day. They passed through the courtyard here (Buckingham Palace) at seven o'clock this morning. We stood on the balcony to see them—the morning fine, the sun rising over the towers of old Westminster Abbey—and an immense crowd collected to see these fine men, and cheering them immensely as they with difficulty marched along. They formed line, presented arms, and then cheered us *very heartily,* and went off cheering. It was a *touching* and *beautiful* sight. My best wishes and prayers will be with them all."

Another example of her intensely English feeling is shown by her reaction to the suggestion that her eldest daughter (the Princess Royal), who was about to marry a Prussian prince, should travel to Berlin for the wedding.

" The Queen *never* could consent to it, both for public and private reasons, and the assumption of its being *too much* for a Prince Royal of Prussia to *come* over to marry *the Princess Royal of Great Britain* IN England is too absurd to say the least. Whatever may be the usual practice of Prussian princes, it is not *every* day that one marries the eldest daughter of the Queen of England." Splendid language in which the reader can almost fancy himself transported back from the stodginess of Victorian England to the robustness of Tudor times.

King Leopold once remarked—and it was very true—that the members of the English Royal Family were nervous and highly strung. To this general characteristic of her race the Queen was no exception. She was excitable. If anything went wrong—and in particular if any friend or relation died—she gave way to lamentations which to-day seem almost eccentric. She looked on death as a personal insult to one who had every right to expect protection from such things. When her mother died, without particular suffering and at the end of a long and happy life, she was prostrated with grief and a fortnight afterwards wrote to explain that she was too broken to endure any " loud talking " and, a few days afterwards, she wrote :

" The blank—the desolation—the fearful and awful Sehnsucht und Wehmuth come back with redoubled force, and the *weeping*, which day after day is my welcome friend, is my greatest relief." (The German words mean Longing and Melancholy.) The reason for this exaggerated attention to death, for indulging in all the trappings of woe and abandoned sorrow, though characteristic of her generation, is not easy to explain. Perhaps Victorian clergymen are in part to blame, for they loved gruesome funeral sermons in which they could describe the once proud human being cast into the tomb, consigned to dust and worms. Churchgoers in those times sang with relish the hymn which contains the lines:

Soon shall you and I be lying
Each within our narrow bed.

The Victorians believed in the terrors of the tomb—in what could fittingly be called the Majesty of Death—and to this dread sovereign they paid tribute in black dresses, made to look dull with never a gleam or glitter of satin or silk, and in

writing paper surrounded with black borders an
inch thick. Therefore the Queen cannot be wholly
blamed for doing what was usual, but it was the
indulgence of grief—almost the enjoyment of it—
which lays her open to criticism. The Prince
Consort once said of her that she lived in the past
and in the future—never in the present. She looked
back with *Sehnsucht und Wehmuth* to the bright days
which had passed, remembering all the pleasant
things which had happened and forgetting what was
disagreeable. She looked ahead to the unknown
and uncertain future with apprehension, contrasting
it with the often imaginary happiness of the past
and feeling that at the best it could only be a pale
reflection of the glories she once had known. As
the Prince pointed out, she never really enjoyed
the present, and that is true of many people with
nervous temperaments. The future daunts them
and spoils the present.

There is one other defect in the Queen's character
which it is important not to overlook in forming a
balanced judgment of her. She was the victim of
extraordinary and powerfully held prejudices. These
were characteristic of one whose point of view was
always emphatic. There is no harm in emphasis
provided it is based on an opinion carefully considered and debated. Too often the Queen's
opinions were based on prejudice and in consequence
she sometimes contradicted herself. For instance

she was very strongly opposed to the marriage of King Leopold's only daughter to an Austrian prince and she wrote to her uncle that it was undesirable because "Austrian society is *médisante* (scandalmongering) and profligate and worthless." Yet the Queen could give this confident pronouncement on Austrian society without knowing many Austrians and without ever having visited their country. A few months later the Princess became engaged to the Austrian and then the Queen—oblivious of her previous indictment of all things Austrian—wrote to her uncle:

" I cannot say how much we like the Archduke; he is charming, so clever, natural, kind and amiable, so *English* in his feelings and likings, and so anxious for the best understanding between Austria and England." John Bright—the great Liberal statesman and cotton-spinner—once remarked that " Ignorance is the mother of prejudice." That is naturally profoundly true and it is certainly right in drawing attention to the prejudices of the Queen to emphasise her readiness to correct them by learning—especially at this period of her life. Here her debt to her husband can never be exaggerated. From the earliest days of their marriage he had striven to form her mind and to draw out her natural gifts and powers, which had not been fully developed by her education. She wrote to one of her closest friends:

" My nature is too passionate, my emotions are too fervent: he guided and protected me, he comforted and encouraged me." On another occasion she said to the Prince, " It is you who have entirely formed me." Some people conscious of the change which was noticeable in the Queen used to refer to her scornfully as " Queen Albertine."

Against the background of these facts, the central tragedy of the Queen's life must be set and studied. She herself was a woman of remarkable constitution —healthy and robust: indeed that was obvious from her appearance—the ruddy face and the firm decided movements. The Prince, on the other hand, was physically not strong though he was a large man. He once said to the Queen, " You cling to life: I do not." In the early winter, following the death of the Duchess of Kent, the Prince became seriously unwell. He was thought to have caught typhoid fever, through a faulty drain at Windsor Castle. Some people have supposed that the Queen (like many people who are blessed with good health) was oblivious to the seriousness of the Prince's state. In fact her diary shows that her worst fears were roused from the first, but she behaved throughout with a high courage which was striking and for one so highly strung was remarkable. She stifled her feelings and was able with complete composure to sit by his bedside, whispering *Es ist kleines Frauchen* (it is your own little wife), as the life of her adored husband ebbed out to its end. To emphasise the magnitude of this calamity for Queen Victoria is superfluous. Anyone reflecting on her happiness, on her reliance on the Prince and on the inevitable loneliness of her position will immediately realise what it meant. As always her own words to her uncle set everything in proper perspective.

" Oh! To be cut off in the prime of life—to see our pure, happy, quiet, domestic life which *alone* enabled me to bear my *much* disliked position, CUT OFF at forty-two—when I *had* hoped with such instinctive certainty that God *never* would part us and would let us grow old together (though he always talked of the shortness of life) is *too awful.*"

* 4 *

Widowhood and Seclusion

IN HIS extraordinary, imaginative and powerful poem—"The Lady of Shallott"—Tennyson draws a picture of this unhappy lady, frenziedly weaving her web and completely indifferent to the bustle and pageantry passing and repassing below her windows. Her solitary existence was alone disturbed by shadows of the great world outside falling across her mirror. So with Queen Victoria. The history of the twenty years of her life, following the death of her husband, is of one living in the twilight, while all the activity and energy of nineteenth-century England passes by her like flickering shadows. In writing to her Foreign Secretary at this time the Queen faithfully depicts her mournful state. She wrote, "The Queen leads the most utterly wretched and desolate life that *can* be imagined. Where *all* WAS peaceful sunshine and perfect happiness (which the troubles and worries of her position rendered very necessary) there is now *utter desolation, darkness* and *loneliness,* and she feels daily more and more worn and wretched."

Yet the Queen was not old: she was forty-two and when her husband died she stood only on the threshold of middle age. She was still active and full of spirit; a few months before his death she and her first cousin (Queen Mary's mother) enjoyed a game of battledore and shuttlecock in the corridor at Windsor. The object of this game played with a small racket, covered with parchment, which lets out a noise as of a distant drum when it struck the shuttlecock—a cork object with feathers stuck into it—was to hit the shuttlecock between the players and to keep it in the air for as long as possible. Its popularity at that time is a proof that Victorian ladies were more energetic than is sometimes supposed. Before that fatal day in December 1861 the Queen was still, as in the days of her youth, fond of dancing; and at Osborne and in the Highlands, she rode and took much exercise. Suddenly with the catastrophe of December 14th, 1861, this active, energetic, determined lady shut herself up, arrayed in all the paraphernalia of Victorian widowhood— thick veiling and black stuff dresses—refusing to be comforted or to take any part in the affairs of the world. Apart from her family, her husband's private secretaries and her ladies-in-waiting or an occasional visiting Cabinet Minister, she saw no one. When she travelled from Windsor to Osborne orders were given that the stations through which she was to pass should be swept of every vestige of humanity. Shortly before the marriage of her second daughter, which took place in the summer after the Prince's death, she was photographed with her elder children: they were all in deepest black: included in the family group was a bust of the Prince Consort, draped round the middle with a garland of roses. The Queen was holding her favourite photograph of the Prince. Naturally it is easy enough to poke fun at the Queen, to ridicule her extravagant mourning—so totally at variance with twentieth-century conduct in the face of death.

She gave orders that nothing in the Prince's rooms was to be touched and so they remained, with his books, papers and clothes all in place until her own death forty years later. It is even supposed that a manservant, each day, solemnly placed a jug of hot water in the dead prince's dressing-room. It is likewise supposed that when she signed important documents of State she looked towards the Prince's marble effigy, which always stood close by, murmuring, in a tone of interrogation " Approved? " Yet in smiling at the Queen, or in criticising her, we should bear in mind that she was bereft not only of a husband but of her guide and counsellor. She explained over and over again to her uncle that the duties and burdens of her position as Queen were only tolerable because of the happiness of her private life, and because of the sympathetic wisdom of her husband

on which she could wholly rely. Both were withdrawn. As her Prime Minister observed in the
House of Commons, " She is left in a solitude of
grief which could not befall any of her subjects."
He meant by that, that Royal persons are cut off
from the consolation of private friendship and in
the case of the Queen this was not balanced by
companionship with her children: she once explained to her uncle that she never felt quite at ease
with them. Therefore she was peculiarly and
tragically alone. In such circumstances each
human being must be left to battle with loneliness
as best they may, and they can reasonably ask, as
they engage in their grievous struggle, to be left
without ridicule or criticism.

For the Queen her one desire was to be left in
peace. She formed a particular aversion for appear-
ing in public, for State functions or for what may be
called the ceremonial side of monarchy. She could
not endure London and for the rest of her reign of
forty years she passed scarcely twenty nights in
Buckingham Palace. In the peace and solitude of
Osborne and Balmoral she alone found life tolerable.
This in itself was a cause of grievance to the statesmen and politicians who had to come to see her on
official business. To get to Osborne they had a
tedious railway journey and the sea-crossing : to
reach Balmoral they had a phenomenally long
journey, which in those days before the invention of

sleeping cars, deserved the description of arduous. Balmoral in particular was appallingly dull—a species of purgatory—for both courtiers and distinguished visitors. At Balmoral the Queen's only recreation was to go out for long drives and it was on one of these excursions, coming home in the dusk, that she was upset in the road owing to her coachman having had an excess of whisky. She was accompanied by her favourite Highland servant Brown, who was on the box with the tipsy coachman: the Queen and her second daughter were inside and a little black boy was sitting behind. They were all tipped into the road and the Queen—who had badly sprained her thumb—was placed in the road with her back to the upturned carriage. The whole episode—alarming and amusing as it was—is most graphically described by the Queen in her book, *More Leaves from A Journal of Life in the Highlands.* She explains—and it is entirely characteristic of her tenacity to life—that while the carriage was turning over she had just time to think of several things she still wanted to do before dying.

But for courtiers and politicians there was nothing to do in the Queen's Scottish home—except for shooting in the autumn months. A Cabinet Minister writing from Balmoral to his wife said, " It is the funniest life conceivable: like a convent. We meet at meals and when we are finished each is off to his cell." Yet it was like a convent with an alarm-

ingly active Mother Superior. She kept everyone
in the castle on tenterhooks. The Lady-in-Waiting,
the Maid of Honour, the Minister in Attendance,
the resident physician, the Lord-in-Waiting, the
Equerry, the gillies, the governors, the private secretary and even the Queen's children—none of them
knew when the dread summons to the Queen might
come nor what they would be wanted for. Nor was
life greatly different at Osborne. On one occasion
she sent for her private secretary and found that
he had gone off to church. At once she wrote a
memorandum to him saying, " This is extremely in-
convenient . . . She must ask Sir Henry to take care
that this does not happen again."

Yet in spite of her grief and retirement the Queen
never relaxed from her work. She argued that it
was the inescapable duty of the Sovereign to master
the often intricate proposals which her Ministers
laid before her. Sometimes she might find it necessary to suggest alterations in them or even to reject
them outright. In his lifetime the Prince had carefully collected and bound in appropriate volumes
all the correspondence between the Queen and her
Ministers, and her diplomatic representatives abroad
and the members of foreign royal families with
whom they both freely exchanged opinions. These
were bound, together with newspaper cuttings and
very often with memoranda setting out his own
ideas on each important issue as it cropped up.

" They are Gospel now " the Queen once broken-
heartedly said after the Prince's death. She meant
of course, by that, that the Prince's papers were to
serve as a guide by which she could continue to
give expression to his point of view. Besides these
tangible reminders of the Prince she was fortunate
in having the benefit of the work of his three private
secretaries—who were all men—trained in public
affairs and marked by good judgment and discretion.
The old objection to the Queen herself having a
private secretary, which has already been discussed
in the beginning of this book, died hard. Although
the Prince's private secretary, General Grey—the
son of the Prime Minister whose Cabinet passed
the Reform Bill—worked in every way as her private
secretary he was not so recognised for six years after
the Prince's death. With characteristic vigour she
wrote to her Prime Minister in 1866 insisting
that Grey should be made her official secretary.
" Every public man has one "—she wrote—" the
Prime Minister has two, and it is perfectly absurd
to *pretend* that the Queen has *none*." Although
General Grey and his successor Sir Henry Ponsonby
did whatever they could to help the Queen there
remained a mass of papers for her to read and to
sign. She liked, whenever it was feasible, to work
out of doors and there are several published photo-
graphs of her wearing a veiled, wide-brimmed hat,
seated at a garden table, toiling away with official

Cabinet despatch boxes beside her. Perhaps the most famous and curious representation of the Queen at work was painted in 1866 by the great Victorian painter, Landseer. The Queen, reading an official paper, is sitting on a pony whose head is held by her confidential Highland servant, John Brown. A Cabinet despatch box lies on the ground. A large dog lies at John Brown's feet, and a little Pomeranian Spitz terrier is sitting up begging by the pony's front legs. While we need not suppose that the Queen often conducted public business on horseback the picture emphasises how the Queen turned recreation and pleasure to business, although she was withdrawn from the haunts of men.

Certainly the Queen was right in feeling that the contribution which she could make to the Government of Great Britain was of essential importance. For example on many occasions it fell to her lot to appeal to her fellow European sovereigns to desist from a line of policy which was thought dangerous to peace. During the years immediately after the Prince Consort's death the Prussians were the great menace to peace and in 1866, shortly before they attacked the Austrians, the Queen wrote the following letter to the King of Prussia and it is clear from the style that it was entirely her own handiwork. She used the formal fraternal greeting, customary between reigning sovereigns, but this did not disguise her affectionate feelings for the King, or the vigour with which she expressed herself.

Windsor Castle, 10th April, 1866

" BELOVED BROTHER,

At this fearful moment I can not be silent, without raising my voice, earnestly, and in the name of all that is most holy and sacred, against the threatened probability of war. It is in your power to avert the calamities of a war, the results of which are too fearful to be even thought of . . . .

War is ever fearful, but when it is begun for mere objects of ambition, for imaginary affronts and wrongs, it is still more fearful. You are deceived, you are made to believe that you are to be attacked, and I, your true friend and sister, hear your honoured name attacked and abused for the faults and recklessness of others. . . .

As you value the life of thousands, as you value the sacred trust, which as a Sovereign you have in your keeping, of maintaining the peace of the world and of promoting the happiness of your own country and of the rest of Germany, and if you have any regard for the memory of him who was your friend (my beloved husband) and for my affection and friendship—pause before you permit so fearful an act as the commencement of a war, the responsibility of which will rest on *you alone*, to be committed.

Q.V.   F

I have ever had confidence in your spirit of justice and, in your Christian humanity, and I cannot, will not, think that I shall have appealed to your heart in vain. Ever your affectionate and unhappy Sister and Friend.

VICTORIA R."

(After the Prince Consort's death the Queen always slipped in the adjective—unhappy—at the close of her letters.)

On political matters the Queen really had no fixed opinions: she was an empiricist in the sense that she decided each question, as she was confronted by it, on its merits. She always regarded herself as Liberal in politics, looking back to her early days with Melbourne and the Whigs as the foundation of her political faith, but she had in fact slight sympathy with the later Liberal measures of her reign. Yet she was not without breadth of mind and though she may not have approved of change, she never tried to obstruct it. In foreign politics she was strongly pro-German—though she bitterly resented it if anyone said so. The reasons for this were obvious—her German relations, the strong German affinities of the Prince Consort and her suspicion of France—a country which throughout the first half of her reign was a source of constant anxiety. Her Uncle Leopold once wrote to her that living next door to Napoleon III was like being in bed with a snake. She shared that point of view.

Unluckily the first considerable crisis in European affairs, which occurred after her widowhood, concerned Germany and it greatly distressed her. It was the question of Schleswig Holstein—one of horrible complexity with its roots going back to the Middle Ages. Fortunately it is not necessary for the average mortal to disentangle them. Even Lord Palmerston, in his jaunty style, said that he did not begin to understand it and that only two people had ever mastered it, adding that of them one was dead and the other was mad. Suffice it to say that these complicated issues gave rise in 1864 to a war between the powerful and rapacious state of Prussia and the small, ill-armed Kingdom of Denmark. English sympathies were strongly for the Danes, especially as the Prince of Wales had lately married a Danish princess. In fairness to the Queen it has to be emphasised that Palmerston and English people generally grossly underestimated the fighting ability of Prussia, Palmerston giving it as his opinion that the French could walk over the Prussian Army. The Queen was anxious, at all costs, to prevent a war between Prussia and England.

The correspondence between the Queen and the Cabinet show her at her most tenacious. She started by saying that she would not willingly give her consent to any course which might involve England in war. Palmerston, in reply, used language which was surprisingly downright. He wrote, " he is sure your Majesty will never forget that you are Sovereign of Great Britain and that the honour of your Majesty's crown and the interests of your Majesty's Dominions will always be the guide of your Majesty's conduct." The Queen was furious, attributed Palmerston's language to a bad attack of gout, and told him that " no feeling for Germany could ever make her view an international question otherwise than as it might affect the interests of the people of England." Palmerston, in a lengthy letter then rode off with a long catalogue of the misdeeds of Prussia adding that that country's behaviour was not " the conduct of brave or generous minds, and it sometimes happens in real life, as it does in romance, that the wicked giant finds that his intended victim meets with unlooked-for support." The Queen icily replied that no good could result from her discussing the relative merits of Germany and Denmark. A few days later she wrote to the Foreign Secretary, Lord Russell, " Lord Russell already knows that she will *never*, if she can prevent it, allow this country to be involved in a war in which *no English* interests are concerned." Russell drily wrote back to her, " Your Majesty is naturally averse to a war in which no English interest is concerned. But if English honour were to be concerned your Majesty would no doubt feel bound to defend it." The Queen replied on the following day, " She must observe that she does not require to be reminded of the honour of England, which touches her more nearly than anyone else." In a letter to her uncle she referred to her Prime Minister and her Foreign Secretary as " those two dreadful old men."

But on May 26th, 1864, the matter was raised in the House of Lords by Lord Ellenborough. This odd but talented nobleman had been the Governor-General of India and he was the author of that punning message, which delighted the Victorians, when he annexed the province of Scinde " Peccavi —I have sinned." His wife, whom he divorced, was also remarkable as she had married a sheikh and lived in a camp near Damascus. He was not lacking in courage and he rose to make a critical speech about the Government's handling of the crisis. In the course of this he suddenly alluded to what he called " a difficulty of the greatest magnitude." He then showed that he had in mind the pro-German sympathies of the Court: he made himself clear by an unexpected panegyric on King George III for having broken the pro-German policy of King George I and King George II. His speech was generally cheered, though the part attacking the Queen was heard in stony silence.

Lord Russell immediately sprang up to defend the Queen, and she wrote to him from Balmoral the next day a letter of warmest gratitude adding, " she must own she thought her terrible misfortunes, her unprotected position without a husband to stand by and protect her, her known character for fearless straightforwardness, her devotion *now* and ever to her country (a proof of which is her weakened health and strength) ought to have prevented *such* an attack—which to a lady she can only characterise as ungentlemanlike." At the same time she wrote a letter, which can most fittingly be described (in the language of slang) as a " snorter," to Lord Derby, the leader of the Conservative Party, to which Ellenborough belonged. She described Ellenborough's attack as " malignant and unmanly " and expressed her regret that Lord Derby, who had been twice her Prime Minister, should have heard it without contradiction or reproof.

Although the Queen's policy was not necessarily right—indeed the subsequent ruthless policy of Prussia and Germany suggests that it was wrong, and that it might have been prudent to give Prussia a knock before her aggressive attacks on her neighbours went any further—it is important to emphasise that her line of policy, pursued with great determination, undoubtedly helped to keep the peace, and to avoid a rash and ill-considered plunge into war. Although the amount of work and correspondence which this crisis entailed was exceptional, it affords a good illustration of her methods of work and is an absolute rebuttal of the idea that she was doing nothing in her retirement.

It was perhaps inevitable that many of her interventions in politics were over trifling issues—especially of course anything which touched her large body of relations. Living so much retired from the world, she was not really in a position to make contributions to vital issues of policy—though she was kept well-informed through her secretaries, and everything she wrote was marked by a sturdy independence and common sense. One of her Prime Ministers was not being idly flippant when he said, " If I want to know what the middle classes are thinking of any measure, I discuss it with the Queen." Like the majority of women her reasoning powers were somewhat wild, and she was inclined to pile on arguments for or against some course of action, where one argument would have been sufficient. An illustration of this is afforded by her discussion with the Foreign Secretary about her second son, Prince Alfred, being considered for the throne of Greece. This throne could not be deemed attractive since the previous sovereign, a member of the Bavarian royal family, had just been drummed out of the kingdom. She started her conversation by saying that " on no earthly account and under no circumstances would she ever consent to it." That was really sufficient to dispose of the matter. But she went on to argue that Prince Alfred's elder

brother, the Prince of Wales, might die without
children in which case he would be King of England:
that he and his brothers might be wiped out by
typhoid fever—an affliction which had lately
befallen the Portuguese royal house: that she would
never allow his children to be brought up as Greeks
and that he was lastly too young.

The kind of issue on which she became suddenly
roused was the danger of railway travel. She
wrote to Mr. Gladstone, " The Queen has repeatedly
written and spoken about this, but she thinks that
nothing has yet been done . . . The Queen's own
family not to speak of her servants and visitors, are
in perpetual danger . . . the Queen is perfectly
determined to *insist* on the subject meeting with the
most serious consideration of the Government."

Her rebukes to Cabinet Ministers, though not
freely given, were severe and conclusive. In 1878
Lord Carnarvon, whose public life had begun when,
as a boy of seven, he made his first public speech
at a meeting of the Society for the Prevention of
Cruelty to Animals, took a different line over the
Eastern Question from that of his Conservative
colleagues. The Queen at once wrote to him.
" . . . The Queen cannot therefore refrain from now
expressing her deep concern, that Lord Carnarvon
should have allowed his personal feelings (which she
is bound to say she *cannot* understand) to find vent
in a speech to a commercial deputation . . . It is

(the Queen must speak *strongly*) lamentable. In conclusion the Queen must say that nothing can give her more pain than to see people, who like Lord Carnarvon, have possessed her esteem and respect, and for whom she has a *sincere regard*, take a view of foreign affairs, or rather more of Eastern affairs and a line of policy, which *she must consider as most* detrimental to the position of her great Empire: and not only to its best interests but to those of the world in general and calculated to prevent peace by encouraging Russia, our worst enemy, in her policy of ambitious aggression and duplicity." A devastating letter to receive. Just as at Balmoral the visitor never quite knew when with a deferential bow, the Queen's personal servant would summon him or her to the presence, so the members of the Cabinet never quite knew when the indefatigable pen of the Queen would be demanding explanations or setting out contrary opinions. As Mr. Gladstone once said, " The Queen alone is enough to kill any man."

Her political views—as indeed must be obvious from the extracts of her letters which have been quoted—were coloured by personal considerations. In consequence when English party politics became a struggle between the two vivid and stupendous personalities of Gladstone and Disraeli the Queen took sides with all her characteristic vigour. Gladstone, whose gifts had been greatly admired by the

Prince Consort, was grave and solemn with something of the same lack of polish in his social manners which had characterised Sir Robert Peel. The Queen had been quick to pounce on this, referring to Peel as " such a queer, odd man." The forthright Lancashire manner and the trace of Lancashire accent which characterised both statesmen, were antipathetic to the Queen. Peel she grew to understand and even admire, but between her and Gladstone the gulf grew ever wider until that last pathetic occasion, when the old man of eighty-five took his leave of her for the last time as Prime Minister, and she could not bring herself either to thank him or to express regret at his going. This was an omission which he felt acutely. The most she could bring herself to say was, in a separate interview with Mrs. Gladstone, that Mrs. Gladstone might tell her husband that she believed he had been very devoted to the throne. Some idea of her feelings for Gladstone are clear from her reluctance to send for him to be Prime Minister at the end of his life although he and his party had been given a comfortable majority in the election. To her private secretary she wrote, " She supposes she will have that dangerous old fanatic thrust down her throat. . . . The Queen can not make up her mind to send at once for that dreadful old man (not because she has any personal dislike for him) as she utterly loathes his very dangerous politics, the language he has held, the way in which he has used every artifice to get in and whom she can neither respect or trust."

None the less it is important to explain why the Queen held these violent views about Mr. Gladstone —since they were not entirely based on prejudices. During his first spell as Prime Minister—that is to say from 1868 to 1874—their relations were normal —certainly better than those between Palmerston and the Queen. The trouble all occurred at the end of the twenty-year period after the Prince's death—towards the end of the 1870's. Disraeli's Government was then in power and was pursuing a vigorous foreign policy over the Eastern Question, as it was then called, which meant the issues arising from the waning power of the once mighty Ottoman Empire. Broadly speaking the policy of Disraeli was to buttress up the Turk as a means of checking the advance towards Constantinople of Russian influence. Russia was a perpetual nightmare to British statesmen in the nineteenth century—largely because of her supposed intention to expand towards India and the East. The situation was complicated by Turkish oppression in the Balkans, which at that time were outposts of the Ottoman Empire. On this issue public opinion—and in particular Liberal opinion—felt very strongly. Then were coined those phrases which have passed into the language " the unspeakable Turk " (this phrase originated with Thomas Carlyle) and the plea that the Turks should be driven out of the Balkans " bag and baggage." The issues might be summed up as a balance between the dangers of Russian aggression and the horrors of the Turkish atrocities. It was on the latter that Gladstone fastened with all the compelling genius of his oratory and the fervour of his righteous indignation.

In justice to the Queen it has to be borne in mind that there was a tacit understanding in those days that foreign politics were not made issues of party politics. But Gladstone attacked Disraeli's Eastern policy hip and thigh—not only in the House of Commons but in speeches up and down the country. Again in justice to the Queen it has to be remembered that in those days Party Leaders were content to make their speeches at Westminster, they did not hold mass meetings in the country except during an election. With that tradition Gladstone completely broke. His progress of speaking reached its height in preparation for the election of 1880 when he was the candidate for Midlothian—the country constituency surrounding the Scottish capital. Here he conducted a campaign, the reverberations of which were almost felt in that haven of peace farther north among the hills of Deeside where the Queen was staying. But there was nothing vulgar or base about Mr. Gladstone's orations—especially as the temptations to indulge in mob oratory must have been overpowering. On one occasion a crowd, calculated to number 20,000, assembled to hear him in the Waverley Cattle Market at Edinburgh. So great was the mass of people that ladies of title on the platform handed down their bottles of smelling salts to revive the victims of the heat and press of humanity. They were almost entirely working men and Mr. Gladstone spoke to them of nothing save the abominable tyranny of the Turks over the Balkan provinces. In these speeches on foreign issues his only device of lighter relief was to make play with the name of some Turkish official—a particular favourite in this connection being the Turkish mercenary soldiers known as Bashi-Bazouks. The Queen felt that not only was Mr. Gladstone stirring up public feeling by these theatrical displays but—and this was of course her principal objection— that they made Disraeli and the Government unpopular abroad and that they encouraged the Russians to continue stealthily advancing in the Balkans. This the Queen expressed very strongly in a letter to the Duke of Argyll in 1877 when war between Russia and Turkey had started.

" My dear Duke,

. . . Though you may refuse to believe statements made by official people, you will not refuse to believe *mine* . . . I wish therefore to state *solemnly* that I know that this war might, and it is my firm conviction *would* have been *prevented*, had Russia not been encouraged in the strongest manner by the extraordinary and, to me, *utterly* incomprehensible, agitation carried on by some members, and especially by one (Gladstone) of my late Government, to believe that she could do what she liked without meeting with opposition. I know this to be true.

Let me add that it is not too late now to act a patriotic part and to desist from so lamentable a course!"

One of the Queen's most decided characteristics was that she held to her opinions about people with the tenacity of a limpet. She never forgot and never forgave Gladstone's conduct in the 1870's. She was further strengthened in this by falling completely under the sway of Disraeli's fascinating personality. Yet this in itself was curious because she had been the first to see, after the Prince's death, the dangers in allowing one individual to have too much influence over her. Immediately after the death of the Prince Consort she wrote to her uncle, "I am also *determined* that *no one* person . . . is to lead or guide or dictate to me. I know *how he* would disapprove it." But Disraeli, in his witty but complete mastery of public affairs, exercised something of the same light-hearted authority over her mind as had Melbourne. He once said to

Matthew Arnold that " Everyone likes flattery ; and when you come to Royalty you should lay it on with a trowel."

But it would be a grave injustice to the Queen and to the Conservative statesman to imply that his position in her affections was derived from flattery alone. He won her confidence gradually —partly because she was amused by him but chiefly because he was always his true self with her. So many people on meeting members of the Royal Family are apt to become pompous or to assume an artificial manner completely foreign to them. This does not pass unnoticed. Disraeli avoided all this by treating Queen Victoria with that blend of wit and banter which had already won him an assured place in the hearts of many eminent ladies. At first she was very much on her guard and wrote in her journal after he had visited her in 1866, " He was amiable and clever but is a strange man." When he first became Prime Minister, which was in 1868, he wrote at once to the Queen. After thanking her he said, " He can only offer devotion. It will be his delight and duty to render the transaction of affairs as easy to your Majesty as possible and in smaller matters he hopes that he may succeed in this; but he ventures to trust that, in the great affairs of state, your Majesty will deign not to withold from him the benefit of your Majesty's guidance. Your Majesty's life has

been passed in constant communion with great
men, and the knowledge and management of
important transactions. Even if your Majesty were
not gifted with those great abilities, which all now
acknowledge, this rare and choice experience must
give your Majesty an advantage in judgment, which
few living persons, and probably no living Prince,
can rival." Certainly this was flattery but in her
reply the Queen brushed it on one side, contenting
herself with an expression of regret that " her
beloved husband was not here to help Disraeli with
his guidance." His next letter, written on the
evening of the same day, was far more characteristic. It was designed to win the Queen's approval
for the appointment as Chancellor of the Exchequer
of Ward Hunt—a rather unknown junior minister.
He starts by agreeing with the Queen that it is
naturally disagreeable for her to have strangers
proposed for high Cabinet office. He then goes on
to get her into a good humour by saying, " Mr.
Disraeli ought to observe to your Majesty that
Mr. Ward Hunt's appearance is rather remarkable
. . . he is more than six feet four inches in stature,
but does not look so tall from his proportionate
breadth: like St. Peter's no one is at first aware of
his dimensions. But he has the sagacity of the
elephant as well as the form." Then he suddenly
switches to a serious note and reveals his true
reasons for wanting this appointment. " The most

simple straightforward and truthful man Mr. Disraeli ever met."

Disraeli only twice stayed at Balmoral, for he fancied himself nervous and bilious there. The fact that he was able to excuse himself from acting as Minister in attendance in Scotland is a further indication of the Queen's affectionate consideration for him. On his first visit he was presented with a full-length photograph of the Prince Consort and in thanking the Queen for this he wrote " he looks upon his relations with that gifted being as among the most interesting passages of his life, nor can he now ever dwell on his memory without emotion." The difference between the personalities of the two great Victorian Prime Ministers is revealed in a flash on considering their relations with the Queen. Gladstone, courteous, correct and despising both fulsomeness and exaggeration, would have found it easier to fly than to express himself in such terms. Nor had he the somewhat gushing and poetic prose style which Disraeli used to captivate the Queen. On one occasion Disraeli wrote to the Queen, who was staying at Balmoral, when he was enjoying the spring in his own country house at Hughenden, " He is not surrounded by so romantic a view as your Majesty. Instead of the foaming Dee, he has a very modest trout stream, and beech woods instead of pine forests. But the scene is beautiful. . . . It is a blaze of bloom and blossom . . . cuckoos in every clump, with the responsive roundelays of wood-pigeons."

But if the Queen was amused by Disraeli she could on occasions smile at him. When she summoned him to form his second ministry, in 1874, he knelt down and, in the words of the Queen in her journal " kissed hands, saying, ' I plight my troth to the kindest of *Mistresses*! ' " The underlining and exclamation mark show that the Queen appreciated the double meaning and was not unmindful of its absurdity.

The influence of Queen Victoria on politics in nineteenth-century England was considerable. While it is true that she never—except perhaps over the Bedchamber crisis in the early days of her reign—came to loggerheads with the Government in the sense that King George III openly quarrelled with Fox and North, she was a potent force, watchful, critical and easily roused to anger. Her influence is not therefore obvious but it was none the less effective. No Prime Minister—not even Disraeli—would have contemplated any important measure without first considering whether the Queen's approval was probable. To that extent her views affected legislation. Cabinets had to placate her—to convert her to their point of view—and it is certainly true that she caused Ministers a great deal of additional work and anxiety.

Reading her large correspondence with Ministers

—swiftly written and not always decipherable with the writing running off into the thick, black margins which edged all her paper—we can see how tireless and active she really was. Any Cabinet Minister was liable to receive one of these letters—full of shrewd questions and giving a point of view which was often refreshingly original in contrast to the one prevailing in Whitehall. Indeed these probing, occasionally encouraging, letters have something in common with the letters written by Mr. Churchill to his colleagues during the war. While readily admitting that Queen Victoria was often a sore trial to her Ministers, all impartial observers would have to agree that she was always prompted by a vigorous patriotic sense, by a solicitous interest in the well-being of her subjects, and she was not influenced by any selfish considerations. This is perhaps most clearly illustrated in a letter which she wrote to a close friend when Disraeli had bought for £4,000,000 the shares in the Suez Canal which belonged to the Khedive of Egypt, " The news of to-day the Queen felt sure must be a source of great satisfaction and pride to every British heart! It is *entirely* the doing of Mr. Disraeli, who has *very large ideas* and *very lofty views* of the position this country should hold. His mind is so much greater, larger, and his apprehension of things great and small so much quicker than that of Mr. Gladstone."

The gifts of character which the Queen showed

in politics were no less obvious in her private life. Although by nature the Queen was warm-hearted and impulsive she was a severe mother particularly with her elder children. But here again this sprang from her own high standard and a longing that they should not fall below the best. Certainly they could never complain that they did not know where they stood with her, for she was invariably perfectly blunt in what she said or wrote to them. She disapproved of what she called lounging in her sons and particularly of too much smoking, card playing, racing and gossip. When all her four sons had been staying with her at Balmoral she wrote icily, " There are too many Princes here at once." When the Prince of Wales was twenty-five, married and with two sons, he wished to go to St. Petersburg for the marriage of his sister-in-law to the future Tsar. After clearly stating why she did not wish him to go, she added, " These are my reasons against it, and to that I may add another, which, dear child, you know I have often already alluded to, viz.: your remaining so little quiet at home, and always running about. The country, and all of us, would like to see you a little more stationary."

She did not at all approve of his racing and she wrote to him, " Now that Ascot Races are approaching I wish to repeat earnestly and seriously that I trust you will confine your visits to the races, to the two days . . . your example can do much for good, and may do an immense deal for evil, in the present day." Much later when the Prince was forty she heard that he was giving a ball at his London house on a day which happened to coincide with the funeral of the Dean of Westminster. She immediately sent him a telegram complaining of his " extreme impropriety." In private she grumbled about his always mixing with " heartless Society people." Of her second son Prince Alfred—a perverse and curious character— she was outspokenly critical. She hated his excessive smoking and gave orders when he was staying at Balmoral that the smoking-room should be shut at midnight and the lights extinguished. When her third son, Prince Arthur, afterwards the Duke of Connaught, acquired a suit with long trousers she at once wrote to his Governor, " She is sorry to see trouser-pockets. The Prince Consort *hated* hands in the pockets, and really to *see* Prince Alfred never with his hands *out* of them would be enough to cure anyone. He walks into dinner and sits at dinner with his hands in his pockets." When Prince Arthur was twenty-eight she wrote to his Equerry, " He must be *dosed* for he is yellow and green."

Her daughters gave her few anxieties, though their matrimonial projects were controlled with a firm hand. When the time for her third daughter (Princess Helena) to think of marriage came round, the Queen wrote to King Leopold, " A married daughter *I* must have living with me." She then went on to explain, in words which might have been used by someone choosing a horse or a comfortable piece of furniture, that she was looking for a Prince, young and sensible, who would not mind making his principal home with her. "Helena —she went on—is so useful I could *not* give her up." Then she added that this eligible Prince must have a small independent fortune, plenty of good sense and must be of high moral worth but it was not necessary for him to belong to a reigning house. In the result the Princess Helena and her two younger sisters all made rather obscure marriages but they and their husbands led happy, useful little lives as appendages to the Queen. If in retrospect Queen Victoria appears a selfish mother, it should be noted that she erred in this respect with the great majority of Victorian matriarchs. Young ladies of the nineteenth century, in choosing their husbands, had to consider their own happiness in relation to that of their parents. A study of the great Victorian novelists would show that a phrase most frequently and most naturally coming to the lips of Victorian young ladies was "Mama wishes me to do this" or "Mama does not like me to do that."

With her sons—the Princes—it was different. For most Victorian women—even mothers of large families—there was something other worldly, almost god-like about men. Sons had to be fêted, indulged and their scatterings of wild oats regretted but accepted as natural behaviour for these amusing, superior beings. From that point of view of her own generation the Queen entirely differed, and in fact she treated her sons far more severely than her daughters. The reason for this—and here she surely showed her natural good sense—was that she was always afraid of her sons developing into a distinctive caste, flattered by well-meaning toadies and consequently spoiled and conceited. She hated royal pride. She made her feelings very clear in a letter to her eldest daughter who had married the heir to the Prussian throne. She started off with characteristic directness in criticising the absurd ideas of rank prevailing in Prussia, and particularly the conception prevalent in that country of the immense position of Kings and Princes. She deplored the way in which Prussian princes mixed exclusively with Army officers because in such circles there was " no *independence* of *character*." She said how she had always tried to instil in her sons the feeling that they were of the same flesh and blood as peasants, working classes and servants, and that was why she had always tried to mix easily with such people as " every respectable lady and gentleman does " in England. She ended—and reading these words no one can fail to perceive the burden of responsibility which she felt in having to guide the early years of manhood of four young men without the help of their father—" It is a terrible difficulty and a terrible trial to be a Prince, *no-one* having the courage to tell them the truth or accustom them to those rubs and knocks which are so necessary to boys and young men."

The picture of the Queen during the twenty years after 1861 is of one manfully grappling with formidable difficulties—striving that her point of view in politics should not be overlooked, roused to boiling point against Mr. Gladstone and constantly anxious over the behaviour and future of her nine children. These preoccupations absorbed her energies. To us living in the next century after her these things are plain. Reading extracts from her journal, her published letters and the lives and letters of many statesmen with whom she worked we can see exactly how her time was passed. Through these publications we can, as it were, walk through the state apartments at Windsor Castle or at Buckingham Palace and boldly enter the Queen's private rooms, watch what she is doing and decide for ourselves what she was really like. Of course she had her faults of character on some of which this chapter has touched. But she would have expected anyone writing about her to be nothing if not frank, and (although she disliked him) she would have strongly endorsed some words of Oliver Cromwell to a famous court painter to whom he was sitting, " Mr. Lely, I desire you would use all your skill to paint my picture truly like me, and not flatter me at all: but remark all these roughnesses, pimples, warts and everything as you see me, otherwise I will never pay a farthing for it." We have the immense advantage of being able to see her as she really was.

To her contemporaries the picture was totally different. They had no means of judging what she was doing. They only knew that she was living a secluded life, and the most they were able to learn from the Court Circular was that she sometimes saw a Minister and regularly went out for drives. But the faultless machinery of Court life ran on. In Buckingham Palace and Windsor Castle fires were lighted with the best coals, thick carpets were swept, stone floors were scrubbed, countless housemaids dusted priceless furniture and pictures, cooks and kitchen maids prepared delicious food, butlers and liveried footmen were attentive ready to answer the bell which never rang. In the stables outside, horses were fed and exercised, painted carriages were polished and burnished but they never formed a procession through excited, cheering crowds. Palace and Castle resembled those penny-in-the-slot machines at seaside resorts. The players are all there —waiting, with characteristic poise, for the master hand to produce the ball and set them into motion. The Queen was adamant : she could not do it.

People began to grumble. In the middle 1860's when the Prince had been dead for some time the newspapers started to echo these grumbles. Her Ministers began to urge her to come to London. Very cautiously and tactfully they asked whether she could not make a particular effort and drive from the Palace to Westminster to open Parliament. Her reply was characteristic. She angrily wrote " to *long* to *witness* the spectacle of a poor, broken-hearted widow, nervous and shrinking, dragged in deep mourning, ALONE *in* STATE as a *Show* is a thing she *cannot* understand, and she never could wish her bitterest foe to be exposed to." *The Times* took up the cry and, in those days, the influence of this journal, both on account of its sources of information and its vast circulation, was overpowering. In a leading article it alluded to the Queen's " unavailing grief " and ended with the statement that people who attempt to live in seclusion have to face a struggle " in which they neither live nor die— neither live, as they wish, in the past, nor do their duty in the working world." To this article the Queen took the extraordinary course of writing a reply, which was published in *The Times* under the heading " The Court." She said that she would do what she could in the way least trying to her health, strength and spirits " but more she cannot do: and more the kindness and good feeling of her people will surely not exact from her." This by no means allayed criticisms. In the cheaper papers there were frequent attacks on the Queen and it was said that on one occasion a placard was hung outside Buckingham Palace which read, " This desirable residence to let—the owner having declined to do any business."

At the same time there was a distinct outbreak of republican feeling. Charles Bradlaugh—an atheist who was later to receive great fame through refusing to take the oath on the Bible which at that time was necessary for every Member of Parliament—went round the industrial towns lecturing in squalid little halls about the iniquities of the Royal Family— especially the remarkable misdoings of the earlier Georges. Joseph Chamberlain—though in a more genteel fashion than Bradlaugh—had also given expression to republican sympathies. Sir Charles Dilke—the son of an old friend of the Prince's and a radical of great gifts—focused attention on the Court in a powerful speech to a crowded meeting in Newcastle. He began by estimating the cost of the Royal Family to the nation, which, at that time, he was able to compute at something in the region of £1,000,000. He attacked the Regiment of Guards —especially the Life Guards—and he caused great laughter by pointing out that, at a recent review of the Life Guards on a Surrey Common, their horses had stampeded, carrying their gallant riders to all corners of the field, because of the unexpected appearance of a flock of geese. He pointed out that an able-bodied seaman was employed all the year round to paint the lion and unicorn on the royal yacht. He computed that thirty-two doctors were maintained to look after the valuable lives of the Royal Family. He ended his speech with a reference to a British republic, " I say for my part—and I believe the middle-classes in general will say—' Let it come.' " He was vociferously cheered. Chamberlain wrote to congratulate him on what he had said, adding, " The Republic must come, and at the rate we are going it must come in our lifetime." Both the Queen and the leading politicians of all parties were greatly shaken—not so much by the speech as by the enthusiasm with which it was received and the indication that such a point of view was not confined to an obscure minority. Mr. Gladstone, who was Prime Minister at the time, wrote to the Queen that the existence of such opinions " is not only matter of grief and pain to Mr. Gladstone and his colleagues, but is also matter of grave public importance."

Two events which were remarkably lucky for the Queen then occurred—although at first sight this might seem rather a curious way of describing them. First the Prince of Wales fell desperately ill, and secondly an attempt was made on the Queen's life. Bad and stenching drains were the common lot in Victorian England and from their evil consequences Princes themselves were not immune. Through contact with one of these death-traps the Prince of Wales caught typhoid fever and hovered between life and death for days in December 1871 —exactly ten years to the month after his father had succumbed to the same disorder. Three times the Queen journeyed from Windsor to Sandringham, expecting on each occasion to see him alive for the last time. The whole nation was on tenterhooks, as each bulletin was published describing the Prince's desperate struggle to live. Slowly but surely he pulled through, and at the end of the following February he and the Queen drove in state to St. Paul's Cathedral to return thanks to God. When she wrote up her journal that evening she said, " I can still hear the ringing cheers, and never can I forget the enthusiasm." It was as she noticed an astonishing, an unexpected display of loyalty. The airy republican visions of Messrs. Chamberlain and Dilke seemed to fade before the full throated roar of London's crowds.

Two days later occurred the most dangerous of the attempts on the Queen's life. She had driven out from the Palace in an open landau and four, and while the police were busy controlling the crowd of sightseers an Irish youth called O'Connor climbed over the spikes on the wall, and slipped into the Palace grounds where he was mistaken for a garden boy. When the Queen drove back into the courtyard of the Palace and was about to get out, she suddenly saw O'Connor, with his hand raised, by the side of the carriage door; she threw herself across her lady-in-waiting calling out " Save me." John Brown leaped off the back of the carriage and Prince Arthur off the box : they caught O'Connor and laid him flat on the ground. Prince Arthur said he thought the youth had dropped something, and, to quote the Queen's own account, " The postilion called out ' There it is ' and looking down I then did see shining on the ground a small pistol." At that time the disturbances in Ireland were at their height and there can be little doubt that O'Connor was seeking, by attempting the Queen's life, to draw attention to the grievances of his fellow countrymen. On the following day she drove from the Palace to Paddington station *en route* for Windsor, and it was noticed that as she drove out from the Palace she got up and stood in the carriage, as an acknowledgment of the extraordinary ovation with which she was received.

Thus very gradually the dark, obliterating shadow which fell across the Queen's life in 1861 began to lighten. One of her great friends, who had been lady-in-waiting to her mother, the Duchess of Kent, was married to the Dean of Westminster. At the end of the 1860's the Queen started going to the Deanery for tea to meet famous writers. She set down in her journal a short account of the people she met gathered together in the Dean's drawing-room—" Mr. Carlyle, the historian, a strange-looking eccentric old Scotchman, who holds forth, in a drawling melancholy voice, with a broad Scotch accent, upon Scotland and the utter degeneration of everything." The historian of Greece —George Grote—and his very ugly wife—known behind her back as The Grotesque—were there. The Queen had known them in old days, thought them unaltered and described her as " very peculiar, clever and masculine." Browning was also there and she called him " a very agreeable man." These eminent persons stood in a row before the Queen and she said that talking to them was " very shy work " but as soon as tea was brought " they talked very entertainingly."

At the end of the 1870's—although she was then nearly sixty—she was even able to dance, and at an impromptu dance at Osborne held to celebrate her youngest child's coming-of-age she danced a quadrille and waltz with Prince Arthur recording with gratification " I found I could do it as well as ever." After this she generally danced at the Gillies ball at Balmoral: on one occasion she danced the Hoolachan (popularly called Hooligan), a rowdy reel with her private secretary. When she was seventy she danced with one of her sons-in-law at Windsor Castle. With surprised approval an observer noted that she danced with " light airy steps in the old courtly fashion; no limp or stick but every figure carefully and prettily danced." A German prince, with a shaky knowledge of English, meaning to say that she danced like a top, declared loudly, " I am agreeable to see that the Queen dances like a pot."

Obviously as the black year 1861 faded farther into the past her naturally happy temperament (and it is easy to forget that the heavily draped widow of the 1860's was the same human being who thirty years before had loved parties, dancing and late nights) began to assert itself. Two things also helped to draw her farther from the shadows—one was her delight in the amusing and entertaining society of Disraeli, and the other was the knowledge, which was so clearly brought home to her in 1872, that in spite of everything she was admired and loved by her subjects. She felt in a curious way that her life had been spared to help the country which she dearly loved. She expresses this in her journal on the thirty-second anniversary of her accession to the throne, " May God help me in my solitary path, for the good of my dear people and the world at large. He gave me great happiness, and He took it away leaving me alone to bear the heavy burden in very trying and troubled times."

* 5 *

Trumpets of Jubilee

DURING THE last twenty years of the Queen's
life her relations with the British people
underwent a subtle, an astonishing change. Yet
she herself altered nothing. She passed rather more
of her time at Windsor Castle and slightly less at
Osborne and Balmoral; her clothes were less
lugubriously black; and here and there her character slightly softened. But she still remained for
long spells in each year at Balmoral or Osborne—
withdrawn but industrious. But the British people,
borne onwards by the flood-tide of commercial
prosperity to vigorous expansion and imperial
acquisition in Africa and the Far East, and towering
above their European neighbours in power and
pride, saw in the homely figure of their Queen the
symbol of all their greatness, the rallying point for
further exertions. How precisely Rudyard Kipling
has given voice to these sentiments! He is trying to
express, in the homely language of a private soldier,
the feelings of the serving men for the Widow at
Windsor, who owns " 'alf o' Creation ":

Hands off o' the sons o' the Widow,
Hands off o' the goods in 'er shop,
For the Kings must come down an' the Emperors frown
When the Widow at Windsor says " Stop ! "

There was something which appealed to the imagination of men, even to the victims of our aggressive policy, in the ordered discipline of the red-coats of the British Army, and the awe-inspiring splendour of the iron-clad warships all seeming to radiate from the black clothes and bonnet of a perfectly ordinary little lady. She seemed in those last twenty years of her life to personify the greatness of England, and to the respect which English people had always felt for her they added a deep sense of pride and affection.

This was manifested at the Queen's first jubilee, known as the Golden Jubilee, in 1887—the fiftieth anniversary of her accession to the throne. The idea that there was something sacred and mystical about the fiftieth year is, in its origin, Jewish. In that difficult book of the Old Testament—Leviticus—will be found the instructions to the Jews about the way they should celebrate the end of the seventh period of seven years, i.e. the end of the forty-ninth year. " Then shalt thou cause the trumpets of the jubilee to sound. . . . A jubilee shall that fiftieth year be unto you." In English history there had been only three English sovereigns

before the Queen to reign for fifty years—King
Henry III, King Edward III and King George III.
The jubilee of King Edward was marked by a general
act of clemency; and the jubilee of King George
by great rejoicings throughout the country, but the
King, whose mind was trembling on the verge of
insanity and whose eyesight was gone, could take
no part in the celebrations except to ride on horseback at Windsor. One lady of ninety-five who lived
in Gloucestershire, was able to appear at the
Queen's jubilee in the same bonnet which she had
worn at George III's jubilee—a beautiful Leghorn
straw in the coal-scuttle shape, fashionable in the
early 1800's. The Queen's advisers—and it was
indeed the wish of all her people—were determined
that the modest celebrations of previous jubilees
should be completely eclipsed by the gaieties of
1887.

The Queen started the rejoicings by a drive to
the East End of London to open the People's Palace,
which took place a few weeks before the jubilee
itself. She was rather annoyed to find that scattered
groups of what she called " Socialists and low, bad
Irish " hooted her, though their efforts were only
here and there perceptible through the deafening
cheers with which she was welcomed. The Home
Secretary—himself Irish in origin and the first
Roman Catholic to sit in the Cabinet—told the
Queen's secretary that, after inquiring among the

escort, he was satisfied that there had never been a more remarkable display of loyalty. Huge streamers were slung across the streets with such slogans as " Welcome as the Flowers In May," " Was There Ever Such A Queen? " and " She is—But Words Cannot Say What She Is."

No more splendid spectacle has ever been staged on the historic streets of London than the Golden Jubilee of June 21, 1887. As the Queen carefully noted in her journal the weather " was beautiful and bright with a fresh air." In consequence the enormous crowds were all in the best possible humour. The procession left Buckingham Palace shortly before 11.30. It started with the carriages of her daughters and daughters-in-law, each with its escort of cavalry. Then came the famous cavalcade of Princes—her nine grandsons and grandsons-in-law, five sons-in-law and three sons. Conspicuous in this group was the Crown Prince of Germany (father of the Kaiser) in a uniform wholly white, having on his burnished steel-helmet the great silver crest of an eagle with outspread wings. No one except his family realised the effort he had made to be there, suffering from an affliction of the throat which made it impossible for him to speak above a hoarse whisper. Within twelve months he was dead. Behind the Princes came twelve Indian officers, in gay coloured uniforms, drawing great plaudits from the crowd. Finally in an open carriage drawn by eight white horses came the Queen, with her eldest daughter and the Princess of Wales sitting opposite to her. She wore a black dress and bonnet, trimmed with exquisite French lace; her jewels were pearls and diamonds; and clearly visible across her breast was the light blue riband of the Garter. In that brilliant and memorable procession she was unmistakably the centre. At Westminster Abbey the procession re-formed on foot, and as she walked slowly up the Nave and came to where the Members of Parliament were standing, she recorded, " I did not see Mr. Gladstone, though he was there." During the service the " Te Deum " was sung to a setting " by my darling Albert." At the end of the service all her male descendants stepped forward and in turn kissed her hand, she embracing each. Lord Rosebery, in a happy phrase describing this act of homage by her descendants, said, " It was history and human nature blended and compacted in a single glowing picture."

She was naturally most deeply moved by the ovation with which she was everywhere received, and she decided to make a public expression of thanks. She began, " I am anxious to express to my people my warm thanks for the kind, and more than kind, reception I met with on going to and returning from Westminster Abbey with all my children and grandchildren." After a reference to her knowledge that the country appreciated what sorrows she had had to bear, she went on, " This feeling and the sense of duty towards my dear country and subjects, who are so inseparably bound up with my life, will encourage me in my task, often a very difficult and arduous one, during the remainder of my life."

One consequence of the Queen's long reign, of her close contact with public affairs stretching back to 1837 and of her great increase of popularity was to make her in politics even more formidable than before. During the last twenty years of her life she had only three Prime Ministers, Mr. Gladstone, Lord Salisbury, who was an Eton boy when she married, and Lord Rosebery who was born when she had already been on the throne for ten years. Her disapproval of Mr. Gladstone underwent no change, and their relations over the disaster to General Gordon were strained to breaking point. The events leading up to the spectacular death of General Gordon admirably illustrate the way in which British influence was spreading; they also show up the sharp difference between the conventional, imperial-minded Englishman (well represented by the Queen) and the less expansive outlook of the Liberal (sometimes contemptuously called " Little Englander "), which Gladstone represented. After the purchase of the Suez Canal Shares, referred to in the last chapter, there was a long period of disorder in Egypt. Finally Gladstone's

Cabinet sent an army, brilliantly equipped and led, which smashed the Egyptians at the battle of Tel-el-Kebir in 1882. The large area to the south of Egypt, known as the Sudan, had long been ruled by Egypt; taking advantage of the weakness of Egypt, a prophet, with a great capacity for leadership, known as the Mahdi, came on the scene and raised the whole Sudan in flaming rebellion. After long debate the Liberal Cabinet decided to send out General Gordon—a fine, fearless and incorruptible Englishman—to evacuate various Egyptian and British outposts in the Sudan. On arrival Gordon decided, on his own authority, to hold Khartoum and the Nile Valley against the Mahdi. The Government hesitated for weeks whether to order Gordon home or to send British troops to relieve him, since he was virtually hemmed in by the Mahdi's troops. Eventually they decided on the latter course and the expeditionary force reached Khartoum on January 28th, 1885, only to find that Khartoum had been stormed and Gordon killed on the 26th. As early as February 1884 the Queen was writing to Gladstone:

" We must make a demonstration of strength and show determination, and we must not let this fine and fruitful country (the Sudan) with its peaceable inhabitants be left a prey to murder and rapine and utter confusion. It would be a *disgrace* to the British name, and the country will *not* stand it.

"The Queen trembles for General Gordon's safety. If anything befalls *him* the result will be awful." Throughout the year she was constantly urging the Government to act, suggesting that Indian troops, accustomed to the extreme heat, might form the relief expedition. When the tidings from Khartoum reached Osborne, where the Queen was staying, she telegraphed in the following terms to her Prime Minister, "These news (she is here using the old-fashioned but not incorrect plural) from Khartoum are frightful, and to think that all this might have been prevented and many precious lives saved by earlier action is too frightful." In ordinary circumstances a telegram from the Queen was sent in cipher so that it could not be read and enjoyed by the post-office clerks through whose hands it passed. On this occasion she took the extraordinary step of sending an open or (to give it its technical name) an *en clair* telegram. The surprise of the village postmistress at Hawarden, where Mr. Gladstone was the squire, as she wrote out this stinging rebuke from the august sender may be imagined. Mr. Gladstone for once was betrayed into loss of temper and said that he would never again set foot inside the Queen's house.

But on the whole the Queen's relations with her Ministers during these last twenty years were kindly —even motherly—rather than severe. This is especially the case in her dealings with Lord Rosebery, the Liberal leader who succeeded Gladstone. When he became Foreign Secretary in Mr. Gladstone's Government of 1886 she told him that she would always be ready to see him and help him, and that she frequently had secret intelligence from abroad which she would be glad for him to see. A few weeks after his appointment she wrote that she was delighted to be able to assist him in his very difficult task " which he had begun so well." When he had become her Prime Minister and was about to make an important speech she urged him to be " as *general* and as vague " as he can be. Lord Rosebery was one of the most versatile and delightful of men. He had once observed that there were two supreme pleasures in life, one real, the other ideal. " The ideal one is when a man receives the seals of office from his Sovereign. The real pleasure comes when he hands them back." While he was Prime Minister he had the astonishing distinction of winning the Derby with his horse Ladas. The Nonconformist wing of the Liberal Party was immediately up in arms against a leader who was successful on the turf, though they never objected when he lost. He said it was absurd to ignore the possession of a few bad horses and then to raise an outcry because he happened to own one good one. Although a peer he was an outspoken critic of the House of Lords. Addressing that eminent body on one occasion he said, " This is not a dissecting room; it is the chamber of death itself." The Queen was always nervous of Rosebery's witty shafts and she once wrote to him that he ought to try to be less jocular. She added, " Lord Rosebery is so clever that he may be carried away by a sense of humour, which is a little dangerous."

During these closing years of her life the Queen's character, softened by the affection of her people, stands out with increasing clearness. We seem, to an exceptional degree, to be able to peer through the façade of Royalty and to see the human being which lay behind. Naturally each person must decide for himself whether the Queen's personality is sympathetic or antipathetic, whether if we had met her we should find her easy or difficult, agreeable or disagreeable. But on one point there is no room for individual decision or for doubt, and that is that she possessed a remarkably forceful personality. Her private secretary once observed that although she was so small, she was always the centre of any company in which she mixed. As soon as the Queen was present, no one had eyes for anybody else.

In the opening chapters of Galsworthy's novel, *The Forsyte Saga*, the reader may recall that clearly drawn and formidable, old lady Aunt Ann, and how the whole of the forceful, vigorous Forsyte family " quailed before her incorruptible figure." Queen Victoria, in relation to her own family circle recalls Aunt Ann Forsyte. Sons, daughters and grandchildren, loved, respected and feared her. Like many heads of large families, she found it easier to show affection to her grandchildren than to her children. This was particularly the case with her eldest grandchild—the wayward, impulsive but deeply affectionate Kaiser. When she first saw him—an infant, just able to totter into the room at his nurse's hand—she called him " Such a little love." She was the only person who could really control him, and he was absolutely devoted to her. One particular episode is an excellent illustration both of the Queen's good sense and of her tact.

During the 1890's the original Dutch or Boer Republic in South Africa—The Transvaal—was under steady pressure from the British territory of Cape Colony in the south and the recently formed British controlled state of Rhodesia (named after the great imperialist Cecil Rhodes) in the north. The situation was complicated by the discovery of gold in the neighbourhood of Johannesburg, in the Transvaal. The lure of this coveted mineral drew crowds of diggers, speculators and murky adventurers to the city. Among them were many British subjects. These new arrivals, and especially the British among them, were not welcomed by the Transvaal Government and its head, President Kruger : they were in fact ill-used. In the closing days of 1895 a small force of a few hundred mounted men, under the command of a Scottish doctor called Jameson, galloped down from the North in an attempt to seize Johannesburg. They were met by Boer commandos—deadly fighters—who hemmed in the doctor and his men, and forced them to surrender when they were fourteen miles from Johannesburg. The Kaiser immediately telegraphed to Kruger congratulating him warmly on the overthrow of " the armed bands which invaded your country as disturbers of the peace." The consternation and indignation in England against the Kaiser after this telegram was boundless: his conduct was regarded as grossly insulting, and a wave of anti-German feeling swept across the country. An influential weekly paper came out with the cry " *Germania delenda est.*" The Prince of Wales wrote to his mother appealing to her to rebuke the Kaiser and, as he said, " to give him a good snubbing." Queen Victoria's good sense was never more clearly shown than in the letter which she wrote to her son. " It would not do to have given him a ' good snub.' Those sharp, cutting answers and remarks only irritate and do harm, and in Sovereigns and Princes should be most carefully guarded against." She went on to say that " William's faults come from impetuousness as well as conceit " and that they were best dealt with by calmness and firmness. The letter which she eventually wrote to her grandson was masterly:

" My dear William, As your Grandmother to whom you have always shown so much affection and of whose example you have always spoken with so much respect, I feel I can not refrain from expressing my deep regret at the telegram you sent President Kruger. It is considered very unfriendly towards this country, which I feel sure it is not intended to be, and has, I grieve to say, made a very painful impression here. . . . I think it would have been far better to have said nothing. . . . I hope you will take my remarks in good part, as they are entirely dictated by my desire for your good." In a long, plausible answer beginning " Most Beloved Grandmama " the Kaiser showed that the rebuke had not been wasted on him.

But the Kaiser was not the only leading German to stand in awe of the Queen. Once when she was in Berlin she summoned Bismarck to see her, at a time when, as " The Iron Chancellor," he was all powerful in Germany and throughout the whole Continent. He was very nervous before the interview, and it was said that he came out, after seeing her, mopping his brow.

In old age she showed many of those flashes of spirit and temper before which even Palmerston and Gladstone had been known to blench. A young member of the peerage was acting as a civil servant and, in the course of business, a specimen of his handwriting came before her. She at once wrote to her private secretary to draw his attention " to this atrocious and disgraceful writing for a young nobleman . . . What would Lord Palmerston have said! " (This was an allusion to Palmerston's handwriting which was perfect, the words rolling off his quill-pen with the legibility of type-script.) There was an air of finality about any reproof from the Queen, which seemed to leave no room for comment or argument. She once wrote to the Prince of Wales warning him against being on friendly terms with Lord Randolph Churchill. After giving her reasons with all her customary force, she added, " Let this subject drop now."

Her own personal attachments remained as strong as ever. To the end of his life her Highland attendant—John Brown—had an extraordinary hold over her affections, and she allowed him to say things to her which she would never have tolerated even from her children. Disraeli once amusingly summed up his power by saying that before he went any further with a certain bill in Parliament he would have to find out the views of the two J.B.'s—John Bull and John Brown. The latter's political opinions were violently Conservative. He thought Gladstone—" that Gladstone " as he always called him—half a Roman Catholic—" We canna have a worse lot." He was very fond of whisky and was occasionally too unsteady to appear before the Queen. She was surprisingly tolerant, and never referred to this failing or rebuked him for it. When Brown died, a member of the Court strolled across to his grave at Balmoral and reflected on the curious fate of this simple Highlander, who was lying in the ground with wreaths from Empresses, princesses and ladies of the Court piled above him. Yet this observer felt that in spite of all his faults and of all the temptations of Court life, he was completely honest. His place was eventually filled by a faithful Indian servant—known as The Munshi, who accompanied the Queen as a kind of personal bodyguard. When she was well over seventy the Queen started to learn Hindustani from the Munshi, and was actually able to exchange a few sentences with Indian visitors to their great surprise and delight.

She kept up her accomplishments—such as music and sketching—till she was quite old. When she was nearly sixty she found great enjoyment in painting the view on a spring evening from her bedroom window at Windsor. After an interval of many years following the Prince Consort's death, she took up music again. But she never went to a public theatre again after the death of the Prince. A lady of the Court urged her to attend a Moody and Sankey meeting. These were two Americans who conducted a number of revivalist meetings in London, helped by sugary hymns written by Moody, with lilting tunes composed by Sankey. " We have reduced the population of Hell by a million souls " they triumphantly claimed. Queen Victoria's response to the invitation was icy. " It would never do for *me* to go . . . it is. the *sort* of religious performance which is not wholesome."

The Queen loved to watch acting, and feeling that it was wrong for her as a widow to go to the theatre, she commanded the *castes* of successful plays to come down to Windsor. In addition to plays, Gilbert and Sullivan's operas, *Carmen* and pieces by the *Comédie Française* were all performed for her benefit. In the winter at Osborne she always encouraged such members of the family as were there and the members of the Court to give private theatricals. She enjoyed these enormously—especially the rehearsing, but it was not thought possible for her to take any part herself. She loved the slow unravelling of the plot, and when there was any surprising development she would turn and say, with an air of triumph, to her neighbour, " There! You never expected that, did you? "

Perhaps the Queen's most distinctive accomplishment was her gift for writing—for expressing herself in words which were simple and vivid and revealed her personality. Her grammar may here and there be faulty, but she had the most valuable gift of all for those who try to write—the power of making her pen say exactly what was in her mind without wrapping it up in elaborate or pompous language.

In his " Essay on Criticism," Pope attacks writers
who cover up their writing with long and intricate
words, in the line, " And hide with ornaments
their want of art." Of that failing the Queen was
never guilty. Many examples of her style could be
given—perhaps the most notable is her description
of the death of two children, by drowning, close to
Balmoral. " Brown came in soon after four o'clock,
saying he had been down at the waterside, for a
child had fallen into the water, and the whole dis-
trict was out to try and recover it—but it must be
drowned long before this time. I was dreadfully
shocked. It was the child of a man named Rattray.
At a little before five set off in the waggonette with
Beatrice [the Queen's youngest child] and Janie
Ely [Lady-in-waiting] and drove along the north
side of the river. We saw the people wandering
along the riverside. Two women told us that two
children had fallen in (how terrible!) and that
' one had been gotten—the little een ' (as the people
pronounce one) but not the eldest. They were
searching everywhere. While we were there the
old grandmother came running along in a great
state of distress." On the following day they went
to see the body of the little child which was lying
in Rattray's house. " Brown went in first and was
received by the old grandmother; and then we
went in, and on a table in the kitchen covered with
a sheet, which they lifted up, lay the poor, sweet

innocent " bairnie," only three years old, a fine plump child, and looking just as though it slept, with quite a pink colour, and very little scratched, in its last clothes—with its little hands joined—a most touching sight. Then the poor mother came in, calm and quiet, though she cried a little at first when I took her hand and said how much I felt for her, and how dreadful it was. She checked herself, and said with that great resignation and trust which it is so edifying to witness and which you see so strongly here, ' We must try to bear it: we must trust to the Almighty.' "

She originally kept her journal, when she was a young woman, as a means of impressing on her mind what she had seen or done. After the Prince's death she used it as an expression of her private feelings, confiding to her journal criticism of her family and matters of that kind which she had formerly discussed with her husband. For this reason, after Queen Victoria's death, her youngest daughter decided to copy out the journal, leaving out these private passages and burning the original. But as many extracts in this book have shown it was not only in her journal but in her letters as well that her gift of self-expression is obviously revealed. On occasion she would herself compose the Court Circular. For instance she used this means to describe her feelings of sorrow at the death of a favourite member of the Court—" The

Queen received yesterday with profound grief the
terrible news of the untimely death of Sir Howard
Elphinstone "; and likewise her feelings of joy when
her great-grandson (the Duke of Windsor) was
born.

As with most of us, increasing years made her
cling with additional tenacity to her personal
fancies. She had a horror of overheated rooms.
When she was known to be about to make an unexpected call on the family of her private secretary,
they spent a feverish few minutes extinguishing the
drawing-room fire with a bucket of water. At
dinner once she started a fierce argument on the
advantage of living at the North Pole in preference
to the Equator; she closed the argument with the
authorative statement that all doctors say that
" heat is unwholesome but cold wholesome." At
a review of volunteers, the gallant men had pressed
somewhat closely round her and she complained
afterwards of the stuffiness. A witty politician
assured her that it was only " *esprit de corps.*"

Her taste in food was simple but particular. She
had a great fondness for a particular kind of German
biscuit and a visitor at dinner once saw her turn
over the biscuits, on a plate in front of her, with
her first finger saying rather sadly, " None of my
favourite biscuits. Do see to it." This implies that
even sovereigns cannot always satisfy their tastes.
An observant peer, who was staying at Windsor,

saw her afternoon tea being carried up. It consisted of a single cup of tea and a plate of sandwiches.
Bearing in this princely repast was the Queen's
personal butler, very old, wearing a white tie and
looking rather like Lord Palmerston. He was
helped by three footmen—gorgeous in scarlet livery
—a surprising quantity of men for a very simple
meal.

Some of her opinions were very strange—or,
perhaps it would be more accurate to say, seem
strange to us in the middle of the twentieth century.
Her views on education would certainly not find
favour to-day; she wrote to her Prime Minister in
1886 that education ruins " the health of the higher
classes uselessly, and renders the working classes
unfitted for good servants and labourers." Hardly
less violent were her views on " Women's rights."
At that time women had no vote, no place in the
universities, no openings in any profession except
nursing and, if they were married, very little
control over their own money. The agitation,
which gained strength in the last twenty-five years
of the Queen's reign, to alter this state of affairs
was described by her as " mad, wicked folly." She
went on to say that one of the leaders of the movement, a titled lady " ought to get a *good whipping*.
It is a subject which makes the Queen so furious
that she can not contain herself." Some people
have argued that a female sovereign, who enjoyed

many of the things denied to other members of her sex, ought to have been the first to welcome this reform. But in fairness to the Queen it has to be remembered that she was always bemoaning her unsuitability as a woman for the burden of sovereignty.

Like many people who are themselves robust, she disliked anything to do with illness and thought it disagreeable and unpleasant to know about the functions of the body. Although doctors were always at hand she was not unduly impressed by them. One evening at Balmoral her physician-extraordinary (to give him his correct title) fell to the ground in a dead faint, during the long period of standing which was customary while the Queen moved round talking to her guests. She asked for an explanation of the disturbance and, on being told, said with a sly little laugh, " And a doctor, too."

She had an infectious sense of humour, with a delightful musical laugh. When she was amused she had a trick of hunching her shoulders—a sure sign that she was in a good humour. She enjoyed telling an entertaining story even if it was against herself. One evening at Windsor, when she was quite old, she looked out of her bedroom to enjoy the night, which was clear and starlit. Immediately below her was the sentry. Hearing the movement above, he thought it must be one of the housemaids and began to address her in most affectionate and endearing terms. The Queen at once drew her curtains but was simply delighted at what had happened, telling the story with great relish. Even in old age the temptation to smile or laugh on formal occasions never entirely left her. She had on one occasion to receive a deputation from the Far East. When they came before her they proceeded to make a series of utterly grotesque and ludicrous gestures—all of course supposed to be respectful and polite. Some of the courtiers, who were standing behind the Queen's chair, could not contain their laughter, and the proceedings were punctuated by their titters and sniggers. The Queen sat apparently unmoved—completely dignified. As soon as the deputation had gone she collapsed into peals of ringing, musical laughter. But through her laughter—and this remark is extremely characteristic—she kept repeating, " But I did get through it all right. I did get through it all right."

Although most of the episodes in the Queen's life and the anecdotes about her which are described here were only made public long after her death, her subjects were able to form some idea of what she was in fact like. They realised that above all else Queen Victoria was intensely human. It was this understanding of the Queen's broad humanity which transformed their affection for her into love— love which was deepened when all could see the

astonishing fortitude with which the Queen faced
the tribulations and disasters of the closing years of
her life. In his beautifully written biography of
Queen Victoria, Lytton Strachey referring to these
last years writes, " The evening had been golden;
but after all, the day was to close in cloud and
tempest."

Certainly the evening or the beginning of the
end, as it might fittingly be called, was golden.
When 1897 dawned her Government and subjects
were agog at the prospect of another jubilee. A
reign of sixty years had never been achieved in
English history, though King George III only
missed this achievement by a few months. The
very name by which the celebrations should be
known created some complexity. A jubilee, as has
been explained, was a period of fifty years. Although
people used silver, golden and diamond to describe
twenty-five, fifty and sixty years of married life, it
was not correct to apply them to a jubilee. The
Home Secretary suggested that the celebrations
should be called " Jubilissime " or " The Queen's
Year " but, as often happens, what was popular
triumphed over what was strictly correct and the
phrase Diamond Jubilee was decided upon.

While it may, on a casual consideration, appear
rather delightful to pass through streets, packed
with crowds cheering themselves hoarse, it is in
fact highly emotional and extremely exhausting.

By 1897 the Queen was seventy-eight, and she felt
that she could not attend a long service and the
fatigues of a ceremonial drive. She also refused to
have any other reigning sovereigns, even her own
grandson the Emperor of Germany. She was
always very particular to show full civility to any
fellow monarch, and she felt that she would be too
tired to give them the hospitality and attention
which she wished to show them. Accordingly the
actual procession was perhaps less splendid than in
1887. As in that year the Queen sat alone on the
back seat in the open, State-landau drawn by eight
cream horses. Facing her was the Princess of
Wales. The Queen's eldest daughter, who had
driven with her in 1887, now had a carriage to
herself drawn by four black horses, richly capari-
soned in red. As she was now an Empress she was
not allowed, by etiquette, to ride backing the
horses which was the reason why she could not
drive in the same carriage with the Queen. The
procession drove to the steps of St. Paul's Cathedral
where a short service was conducted by the Archbishop of Canterbury. The return was by London
Bridge and the populous streets south of the Thames.
It would be tedious to describe the density of the
crowds and the deep roars of cheering with which
the Queen was received. With touching simplicity
she wrote in her journal, " No one ever, I believe,
has met with such an ovation as was given to me."

Undoubtedly she was right. The cheers which welcomed King Charles II to London on that day in May 1660, the vociferous applause given to Napoleon on returning to Paris after one of his victories, or the acclamation received by some emperor of old, celebrating his triumph in the streets of Rome, would have sounded weak and watery in contrast to the cheering in London on June 22, 1897. It was said that, through the cheering, the Queen heard a rough man call out at the top of his voice, " Well done, old girl." She was delighted.

As some compensation for the lack of colour and splendour in the procession, caused by the absence of foreign rulers, representatives of the Empire were given great prominence. The jubilee of 1897 was an imperial occasion. This was singularly appropriate, for the most spectacular change in the sixty years of the Queen's reign was in the growth of the British Empire. The tough islanders of 1837, with their colonies and dependencies, had merged into a vast Empire with one quarter of the habitable globe splashed red. At the beginning of the reign politicians of all political parties looked on the colonies as burdens, as mill stones round the neck of the mother country. By the end of the reign, Canada, India and Australia were unified and capable of self-government. During the reign huge tracts of country in Africa, Burma and Malaya had come under the British flag. The first colonial conference was held in London in the 1880's and from that beginning started the origin of the idea of the British Commonwealth of Nations. Some Liberals and progressive thinkers strongly objected to this painting the map red and to the savage fighting which too often accompanied it. They were however in a minority, and the majority saw themselves as a Chosen People whose duty it was to rule " the lesser breeds without the law." These were Kipling's words in his " Recessional," which was written in Diamond Jubilee year, and he was likewise responsible for the description of our Empire as " The White Man's Burden." To-day we may look differently on such matters, but it has to be remembered that there was hardly a family in the British Isles which had not been personally affected by our great exertions to expand. Throughout the sixty years of the Queen's reign there was a succession of small wars—at the beginning the struggle to establish a foothold on the fringes of China, in the middle the great disorders in India culminating in the Mutiny, and at the end the long succession of battles in Africa. In this fighting, or in the sickness which claimed as many British lives as did the primitive weapons of the natives, the Queen herself lost one of her grandsons and her son-in-law. Few families of the well-to-do or middle classes escaped these losses as is obvious to any visitor to our churches, glancing at the memorial brasses on the walls or the tattered flags, hanging in our cathedrals or town churches. The middle classes sent many of their sons to administer the government in India, and from Scotland and the industrial towns there was a constant stream of emigrants to Canada and to Australia. In all these exertions, which touched Englishmen most nearly both in their pride and in their affections, they saw the Queen, whose life had been so astonishingly prolonged, as the symbol of success—someone on whom they could fasten as living proof of their brilliant and spectacular achievements.

But as the chilling words of Strachey remind us, the glory of the Queen's reign was to be obscured at last by cloud and tempest. Johannesburg was still the centre of disturbance. President Kruger, who was still head of the Transvaal state, was obstinately anti-British and refused to lighten the severities with which the British were treated in Johannesburg. The two countries drifted towards war which finally broke out in October 1899, the Orange Free State joining with Transvaal. Great Britain had some ten to fifteen thousand regular soldiers in South Africa: Kruger could rely on a Boer force of 50,000. British defeats quickly followed. In the week beginning December 10th, 1899, there were three major disasters to British arms, and the period was ever afterwards known as " Black Week." The Christmas of 1899 was the most grim of the Queen's reign, and she wrote in her journal on January 1, 1900, " I begin to-day a new year and a new century, full of anxiety and fear of what may be before us." Yet her spirit was unbroken. When a leading politican went to see her at the beginning of 1900, he began the conversation by lamenting the grievous reverses of Black Week. The Queen cut him short, and said, " Please understand that there is no one depressed in *this* house: we are not interested in the possibilities of defeat. They do not exist." And when the German Emperor telegraphed to say that the Germans would be very glad to try to arrange terms of peace between the Boers and England she answered, " The time for, and the terms of, peace must be left to our decision, and my country, which is suffering from so heavy a sacrifice of precious lives, will resist all interference." After the news came of the relief of Ladysmith, where British troops were closely besieged by the Boers, she drove in state to the City to express her gratitude for the way in which the City of London had supported the war. She was quite taken aback by the warmth of her reception which she said was " if possible, even beyond that of the two Jubilees."

She had for the last few years spent the early spring in the South of France, at Cimiez on the French Riviera, but because she and her country had been attacked in the Paris papers she decided not to go in 1900, but to pay a visit to Ireland where she had not been for forty years. She did this for the sole reason of showing her gratitude to the Irish for the way in which they had rushed to fight against the Boers. She also agreed to the formation of the Irish Guards and allowed members of the various Irish line regiments " to wear the green " (that is a piece of shamrock) on Saint Patrick's Day. In conversation with the British Ambassador in Berlin after his grandmother's visit to Ireland, the Kaiser said, " Her Most Gracious Majesty has the wonderful gift of always doing the right thing at the right moment." In Ireland again her reception was overwhelming and she noted in her journal that the Irish form of cheering was more shrill than in England, approaching a yell. But the exertions of this visit to Ireland were too much for the Queen. She admitted this on getting back to England saying, " I had a great deal to get through, and I was so anxious that everything should pass off well."

During the summer she failed noticeably though she continued to work. At the end of 1900 she managed to struggle to Osborne for Christmas but she could neither eat nor sleep, and was condemned to a diet of slops which she bitterly lamented. In the middle of January 1901, with the unsettling sensation of a distant roll of thunder on a peaceful morning, the news reached the public that " The Queen has not lately been in her usual health."

Three days after this bulletin was published she died, surrounded by her children and grandchildren, and it is said, supported to the last by the arm of the Emperor, who had dashed from Berlin to be with her before she died. She was laid out, after death, wearing her widow's cap and a bridal veil —the symbols which recalled the Prince—the greatest influence in her life—and reminded all who saw her of her crowning happiness and crowning sorrow.

Her coffin was brought from the Isle of Wight to England in the royal yacht and as the small vessel, escorted by destroyers, passed the huge battleships of the Fleet, it was received with a thunderous salute. Those who witnessed this tremendous spectacle were reminded of those astonishing developments which had taken place during the sixty-four years of Queen Victoria's reign. In 1837 the Navy had wooden ships and "the wooden walls of England" was a saying still literally true. In 1901 wood had given place to iron and steel, sail to steam and the submarine had been added to the Fleet. When the Queen came to the throne the only main line railways were the Great Western to Bristol and the North Western to Birmingham. By 1901 railways covered the land like the lines on the palms of the human hand. Electric traction—to give trams their correct if somewhat pompous name—was transforming town life: the motor car was on the fringe of popularity when the Queen died, and the bicycle was everywhere by 1900. Mr. H. G. Wells wrote his delightful fantasy about the bicycle, " The Wheels of Chance," in the year before the Diamond Jubilee. The telegraph had been perfected during the Queen's reign and the telephone was becoming popular when she died. She herself listened to it at Osborne when a concert was relayed for her from the neighbouring town of Cowes, and she also heard a bugle played from Southampton and an organ from London. She thought it " sounded charming " though the organ came through very weak. The gramophone was also invented in her reign, and in 1898 she made a recording of a message to the Emperor of Abyssinia—the King of Kings or Negus Negusti as he was called. The message began, " I, Victoria Queen of England hope your Majesty is in good health." The record was then sent to Abyssinia and played through to the Emperor and his Consort. The Emperor stood while it was being played, and a salute of artillery was fired.

But if these were some of the more striking and spectacular advances of the Queen's reign, it is also the fact that man's whole life inside his home and outside had been revolutionised by the great discoveries of her reign. There was hardly any sphere of life from kitchen ranges, electricity and gas to public displays of football and cricket where man's existence had not been simplified or made more agreeable by the progress of invention. These changes give the reign of Queen Victoria its importance in the pages of history. But yet neither they nor the great political, military and imperial events of those sixty-four years ever succeed in dwarfing the character and personality of the Queen. It is in *her* reign, *her* age that *her* people achieved these wonders. Was not she herself almost as wonderful as the changes and inventions through which she lived? Certainly many ordinary mortals thought so and would have agreed with the sentiment of that simple Zulu chief who, when he heard that the great Queen Victoria had died, said, " Then to-night I shall see another star in the sky."